CARL NIELSEN

One of the last photographs

CARL NIELSEN

SYMPHONIST

1865–1931

by

ROBERT SIMPSON

With an introduction by
H. E. COUNT REVENTLOW
Danish Ambassador in London,
and a biographical appendix by
TORBEN MEYER

Illustrated with photographs
and musical quotations

LONDON
J. M. DENT & SONS LTD

TO MY FRIENDS

IN THE

DANISH STATE RADIO SYMPHONY ORCHESTRA

INTRODUCTION

IT HAS been a great experience to me during my long tenure of office in London to witness the growing British interest in Carl Nielsen.

He had deep roots in the Danish countryside; he drew his strength and inspiration from its people and nature, and it may be that it was this his Danish originality which for some time made it rather difficult for others to appreciate his music. However, as soon as the Danish State Radio Orchestra had the opportunity to interpret his symphonies in Edinburgh and London, he was widely acclaimed as one of the great composers of this century.

There is now an insistent demand for factual information about Carl Nielsen and his music, and I therefore welcome this concise survey which so well answers most of the questions asked. The author and the publishers are indeed to be congratulated on their fine work.

REVENTLOW,
Danish Ambassador.

CONTENTS

ILLUSTRATIONS

PHOTOGRAPHS

IN THE TEXT

FOREWORD

THE first impact of Carl Nielsen on English-speaking listeners has been as a symphonist; his symphonies may be heard on the gramophone and radio, and the pocket scores are obtainable with reasonable ease (not, as yet, No. 6). Fortunately the series of six symphonies, properly understood, forms an excellent basis for a study of his work as a whole. That is why I have made it the central substance of this book. As Bernard Shaw said about the old Philharmonic Society: 'They once, as all the world knows, got Wagner, who, with the strong common sense to which he then owed his reputation as an unpractical madman, told the directors that their programmes were too long, and that no conductor could do better for them than make his choice between thoroughly rehearsing one or two things, leaving the rest to tumble through anyhow, and having everything only half prepared.' The entire concert of Nielsen's works sets a writer this selfsame problem, but the conditions are luckily more favourable, and I hope that the chapters on the rest of his music do not 'tumble through anyhow.' These sections (as well as Torben Meyer's biographical appendix) are essential to the complete picture: this composer is far from being only a symphonist, and all his major works are given consideration. A writer is better off than a conductor: he can rehearse to at least his own satisfaction. His problem is not time but space. I do not, however, believe that to leave everything half done is the right way of showing the depth, power and subtlety of which Nielsen is capable as an artist, and I therefore make no apology for the detailed treatment of the symphonies. Most readers who can play the gramophone will have little difficulty in following the analyses, and experience as a W.E.A. tutor has taught me that the average intelligent music-lover is able to gain an astonishing degree of familiarity with large-scale works. The question of tonality (or key) is so fundamentally important in Nielsen that I have not hesitated to tackle it in the knowledge that to grasp it (a much less difficult task than some think) is to win very real rewards. An understanding of the symphonies does, in fact, illuminate all the other works, and the following essays on them are meant to be of use to the student as well as the concert-goer or gramophonist.

Two important works that I have regretfully had to tumble through are the operas (discussed briefly in Chapter XII). These can be adequately treated only with more music examples than the most generous publishers could allow in these circum-stances, and I would not presume to assess their effectiveness as stage works without yet having had the luck to see them on the stage, though I can vouch for their musical value. The evidence is all in favour of their being successful on the English stage: fuller discussion of them will be possible after that event.

Danish readers may find a little strange at first the frequent dropping of the 'Carl' from the composer's name, since the use of both names has become a necessary habit in Denmark where Nielsen is almost the commonest surname. In England this is not necessary, and might even (if continually repeated) seem somewhat pretentious to English ears: so I trust that those who are used to saying 'Carlnielsen' will not feel that this book is about the wrong composer.

At the end of each of the chapters on the symphonies I have included a brief list of contemporary works by other composers; this is not intended to be in any way exhaustive, but merely to serve as a sketched background. The works are not listed in any special order, nor are their exact dates given; their haphazard order may, perhaps, enhance the charm of contemplating the hotchpotches they make.

My sincere gratitude is due to the following: to Mrs. Irmelin
Eggert Møller, the composer's elder daughter, for her great
patience in providing me continuously with all kinds of
essential material; to Eric Blom for kindly reading the proofs
and making valuable suggestions; to Count Scheel for his
ready assistance and good offices; To Torben Meyer for his
cooperation; to my friend Harald Knudsen, whose tremendous help as translator became a *sine qua non*, and whose
enthusiasm has at all times enlivened mine; to Renée Oliver,
for saving me much of what she called (a shade too zoologically) 'donkeywork'; to Ruth Lachmann for helping to
make the Index; to Alan Collingridge for his very real
encouragement at the start.   I am also grateful to Mr. Launy
Grøndahl for kindly allowing me to use Carl Nielsen's letter
to him (reproduced on p. xvi), and to Messrs. R. P. Keigwin
and Basil Blackwell for permission to print the former's fine
translation of *Jens Vejmand* (pp. 173–4), published by the
latter.   For many useful and stimulating discussions I owe
much to Tony Dorrell, and lastly must come the inevitable
tribute to my wife's stoicism in hearing the whole book read
from end to end.

R. S.

London, March 1952.

27 - 6 - 26

[handwritten letter in Danish, signed Carl Nielsen]

Translation:

DEAR MR. LAUNY GRØNDAHL!

You can be sure I was very glad to receive your greetings on the 9th June [1] and also to hear, at a long distance, near Fredericia, your and the radio orchestra's performance of my works. I thank you many times from the heart and beg you to repeat my regards and thanks to the orchestra.

With kindest wishes I am,
Yours affectionately,
CARL NIELSEN.

[1] C. N.'s birthday.

CHAPTER I

THE GROWTH OF THE ARTIST

AN artist is not self-made. As Carl Nielsen's almost complete opposite, Gustav Mahler, once said: 'We do not compose——we are composed.' Heredity, human and scenic surroundings, immediate circumstances, world situations, all these things, though a man may radically influence them, he cannot singly control. His reactions to them emerge from the interaction of his reason with his temperament; the former disciplines the latter, but is not free to develop itself unless the temperament allows. A man's art is his considered verdict on life, and must be judged by what it omits as well as by what it contains; yet the greatness of an artist depends rather on what he is than on what he is not. No artist can be genuinely great unless his criticisms of life are positive and constructive. And it follows from this that his creative impulse must needs be directed by high powers of organization, for if it is to reflect life, it must convey a sense of purposeful, organic growth. Thus great art, whether it treats of comedy or tragedy, life or death, is essentially hopeful, objective.

The main burden of this book is to show how Nielsen's life-work sprang from his instinctive search for an objective view; how he did not always achieve it, and how those works in which he did are invariably more finely wrought, how the organic nature of his best music identifies form with content, and how the steady growth of his humanity is faithfully reflected in the main trend of his artistic development. To see all this clearly two approaches are necessary; the general and the closely analytical, both equally important, and the most difficult to set out lucidly is the latter. Nielsen's six symphonies give a clear

B   I

outline of his career; detailed treatment of these will make it possible to deal with the rest of his many-sided genius in a more general way.   After this, wider conclusions can be drawn.

Carl Nielsen was born a peasant, and his first experience of music was of the simple songs and dances of his native Fyn. Danish folk-music has a very individual flavour; it is uncom-plicated, though often irregular in metre, its melody is naturally of Teutonic cast, but it never plods—it always strides or flows; it has the true Nordic clarity of outline, with a certain bluntness, yet it can be gentle and soothing in a very masculine way. One quality that is almost never found in it is sentimentality, and in its freedom from this it has more in common with Norse than with Swedish or German folk-music.   However much Nielsen learned about the art of music from his experi-ences in Copenhagen and other great capitals of Europe, from his study of the musical classics, and whatever the width of culture he obtained from his comprehensive reading, he never ceased to regard the music of the Danish villagers as the basic nourishment of his work.

Later he gleaned much from Gade and Svendsen, who encouraged his already growing sense of composition: he developed an enthusiasm for Brahms, and for Bach and Mozart.   It must not be forgotten that he was born into a time when musical romanticism was at its height, and it is as well to pause and define the term 'romantic' as it will be used in this book.   There never was a more loosely used term.   The revolt in the latter part of the eighteenth century was not against 'classicism,' but against a moribund and routined order of things: individualism had to assert itself against the dead hand of mannered convention.   The world lives by the infinite variety and corporate vitality of its individual minds; such a revolution was healthy and realistic.   Inevitably the pendulum swung too far, and as the next century progressed, artists began to think so much of individuality that, in order to maintain their illusions, they started to 'romance,' to make up stories about life. It is in this sense that the term 'romantic' is applied here, not in its usual misleading opposition to 'classical,'[1] but in its old meaning. The romanticist, in this sense, never gives a really truthful account of his feelings; there is an element of egotistical exaggeration in everything he says. This is not to aver that all nineteenth-century artists belong to this school, but it is to describe the kind of thought from which Nielsen turned away. He was never an 'anti-romantic¸ (that is a kind of neuro-tic), nor was he a 'classicist' or 'neo-classic' (these are afraid of life): at his best he may be described as a life-sized artist, exact in the representation of his thoughts. He subscribed to no school, but expressed himself with scrupulous truthfulness.

The Brahmsian element in his first period is the result of his feeling that Brahms was the most firmly disciplined master of his time; what he derived from Brahms was a powerful sense of construction. The German's romantic traits he discarded; from the beginning he was incapable of even a trace of senti-mentality, and he had an alert Mozart-like way of analysing a man's character—his admiration of Brahms, for instance, did not fog his vision when he met the great man. Here is his almost uncanny description:

Brahms is of medium height, very squarely built, stands steadily and firmly on the legs and makes the impression of having great strength. He is very short-necked and a bit stooping, and if one sees him from the back, the head sits between the shoulders and the back is slightly rounded. His expression changes during the conversation, and now the eyes have a sarcastic, nearly vicious glance, now they become infinitely hearty and good. Much is said about his nasty tempers, and I can quite believe he could be frightfully biting, but then there are so many aggressive people, and I'm certain that it's only to that sort he gives the whip.

This fascination for human character is the key to the under-standing of Nielsen, and it springs from his essentially generous

[1] An equally meaningless term.

outlook. Its progressive development may be seen in the first five symphonies, and it is discussed more fully in Chapter XIII. And there is no paradox in the fact that the wider and more selfless his attitude became, the more striking was the individu-ality of his style: a generous personality always makes a stronger impression than a circumspect one, and an artist who strives desperately to foist his individuality at all costs finds in the end that he has only the costs left. Nielsen's style is full of 'fingerprints,' rhythmic, melodic, contrapuntal, harmonic, and tonal, and there is no point in trying to list them here; the reader will be better occupied in noticing them for himself as he listens to the music. Although such things as the flattened seventh (the clear influence of folk-music), the swinging athletic triple time, the amazingly simple yet original use of major and minor thirds, and numerous other characteristics will become familiar, the music is never restricted to a stylized affectation; there seems to be no limit to its range and power. Those who feel its influence are not forced into the confines of a cult; its breadth and freedom have a releasing effect on the mind.

As he matures, Nielsen moves further and further away from stereotyped forms; his greatest and most far-reaching mastery is of tonality, and at a time when most other composers were losing their grip on this element, he was discovering new significance in it. The so-called 'disintegration' of tonality in the first twenty years of this century is in reality a disintegra-tion of composers' ability to use it in fresh ways; impotence became the fashion, and in the name of adventurousness, many gifted musicians threw to waste what they would not give time to understand, while others, attempting to conceal their own exhaustion, asserted that tonality was played out. Nielsen, alive to all this (he travelled extensively and met most of his distinguished contemporaries), quietly gained a deep insight into tonality that saved him the embarrassment of trying petulantly to kick it to pieces. Like all really original minds, he flouted tradition only by reacting naturally to all the funda‑ mental facts on which it is based, and he soon found a totally new way of regarding these facts.

Already in the first Symphony his boldness is apparent and his handling of keys is new, and it was to become a positive principle with him that a sense of achievement is best conveyed by the firm establishment of a new key. In the third, fourth, and fifth Symphonies this principle is expressed with remark‑ able subtlety, force, and depth, as the following analyses should show; and it is interesting to see that in his last period, when he wants to create a sense of unresolved conflict, he makes his clarinet Concerto struggle vainly to escape the toils of a fixed key, in which it ends. In the great first movement of the sixth Symphony, he produces a tragic effect by the opposite means; the music tries constantly to return to the idyllic G major where it began, but succeeds only in establishing the keys a semitone on either side of it—so near and yet so far. The only other of his contemporaries to hit on this device of 'pro‑ gressive' tonality on a large scale was Mahler, who used it with impetuous vigour and originality in his second, fourth, fifth, seventh, and ninth Symphonies, often with deep poetry and impressiveness, but never with the cogency and concentration of Nielsen. The Danish composer developed a dynamic view of tonality; most of his mature works treat a chosen key as a goal to be achieved or an order to be evolved, and his final establishment of the key has all the organic inevitability and apparently miraculous beauty with which the flower appears at a plant's point of full growth. This way of thought has infinitely wider possibilities than the so‑called 'atonality' or 'pantonality,' and it may well bring into modern music that healthy sense of structure so much of it lacks.

As with most other composers it is possible to divide Nielsen's career roughly into periods: the first ends with *Saul and David* and *The Four Temperaments* (Symphony No. 2), about 1902–3 (including the *Helios* overture); the second begins with the bold choral work *Sleep*, contains *Maskarade*, and culminates in the *Sinfonia espansiva* (1911); this second period is the sunniest in his whole life, filled with a Jovian sense of well-being. The third period may be said to open with the Sonata No. 2, for violin and piano, and the main works between 1912 and 1922 show a new quality of steely determination whose climax is the overwhelmingly powerful fifth Symphony, perhaps the highest of all his attainments; a delightful appendix to the third period is *Springtime on Fyn* and the wind Quintet. The fourth and last period, which includes the sixth Symphony, the concertos for flute and clarinet, the three *a capella* motets and, above all, the splendid *Commotio*, for organ, finds him exploring new lands. His polyphonic technique becomes more and more sensitive: some commentators have suggested that the sometimes pungent sound of his music at this time (Symphony No. 6, *Preludio e Presto* for solo violin, clarinet Concerto, and the extraordinary three pieces for piano, Op. 59) is due to the influence of Schoenberg, but nothing could be further from the truth. There is no connection between these two composers, either in spirit or in technique, and the originalities of Nielsen's last period are latent in his own early works. This fourth period has a transitional character, and its strangeness is the result of his isolating stylistic features that had hitherto appeared only intermittently. In no way can this period be considered a philosophic summing-up in the sense that Beethoven's last quartets present themselves.

Nielsen's last years were beset by an emotional upheaval that arose partly from his distressing heart trouble and partly from his growing sense of foreboding about the state of the world; this disturbance in his spirit he managed largely to conceal in his daily life, as he also did his best to prevent his illness becoming apparent. But its effect on his music, especially on the sixth

Symphony, is marked: between the fifth and *Commotio* there is no work to which, as a whole, the word 'greatness' can be unhesitatingly applied, unless one admits the penetrating clarinet Concerto into that category, while the flute Concerto is so rich in human sympathy that its plea, too, is more than persuasive. All these works, however, belong to a transitional phase, and it is both inspiring and saddening to contemplate the serene grandeur of *Commotio* and to realize that this is not the end of the fourth period, but the beginning of a fifth, a great stabilization. But it is good to know that in his last great work he achieved once more a profoundly affirmative note.

CHAPTER II

THE FIRST SYMPHONY
1891–2

By 1891 Carl Nielsen had composed very little for orchestra, but although the only earlier scores that remain are the Suite for strings and the unpublished *Symphonic Rhapsody*, the symphony shows no sign of inexperience. The originality of its tonal structure is something that might have occurred to him at almost any stage in his career, and the technical adroitness with which he carried it out suggests that he must have des⁄troyed many preliminary studies in orchestration. His debt to Brahms is often obvious, though his scoring, with its open bluntness of sound, is more like Dvořák's; the personality expressed, however, is his own from start to finish. Not even his late work is more characteristic of him than the first Symphony. It is a common fault of criticism to pay more attention to the influences of other composers in a young man's work than to its own character as music. Certainly some young artists succeed only in imitation, and if they self⁄con⁄sciously try to avoid the impact of older and more experienced minds, fail to find even a synthetic character of their own. But in his twenties, Nielsen had strong views: his attitude led him away from the romantics, and the architectural mastery of Brahms appealed to his natural desire for objectivity. He realized at the beginning that no one with a real character need fear to learn from another man; all that can be expected of any artist is that his nature should express itself truthfully, as it is, at any given time in his life, and it is in this sense that the G minor Symphony is a truly typical work. It sums up the whole of the man as he was in 1892. Thus it can, as a work of art, in no way be called immature, and it is important to remember that he himself always refused to look at it in the way that so many composers, in later life, regard their early music. He always asserted that, whether it deserved criticism or not, it remained to him a true statement of what he felt when he wrote it. So there is no reason to make excuses for it; he wanted it judged on its own merits, without reference to his later achievements.

At the age of twenty-six Nielsen was, of course, elated by his sense of growing powers, and the first Symphony is a bold and deliberate assertion of his individuality. Its tonal scheme is extremely daring, and it is possibly the first symphony to end in a key other than that in which it started. Mahler's second Symphony, which opens in C minor and closes in E flat, came three years afterwards in 1895, and those two keys are quite closely related in an orthodox sense. The two keys Nielsen chooses are G minor and C major: in this respect he is far bolder than Sibelius, whose first Symphony (seven years later) is a romantic work laid out on fairly conventional Tchaikovskian lines. Sibelius's attitude to tonality remains conservative throughout his seven symphonies, and his originality and mastery in the use of this profoundly important element would have to be analysed in a totally different way. The two temperaments are almost diametrically opposed and further mention of this question may be found in Chapter XIII. Nielsen's decision to connect the keys of G minor and C major could not, for him, have been a difficult one to make. His long and close proximity with folk-music made the major scale with a flat seventh (the so-called Mixolydian mode) quite familiar to him, and it is also typical of his sunny disposition that when he composes in a minor key, the minor third may behave without warning as if it were a flat seventh in a major key.[1] It is a thing that Haydn, had he lived in Nielsen's time,

[1] In this case the note is B flat—the minor third in G and the flat seventh in C.

would almost certainly have done habitually. One finds it
frequently in the English 'pastoral' school, though the tendency
is more often reversed (the flat seventh in major becoming a
minor third), and it is there often the product of a cult. In
Nielsen's music it is to be found in its natural, unsophisticated
state, as part of his style: the first Symphony raises it to the level
of a principle. The tendency to move away from G minor to
C major is the basis of the whole structure, and one can
imagine the startling effect at the first performance in 1894 of
the sharp opening chord of C major, suggesting an uncomplicated brisk cheerfulness, being suddenly obscured by a stormy
G minor.

The breadth of this composer's conception is immediately
shown by the fact that this quotation is the start of a 20-bar
sentence for the full orchestra (except the trombones which,
in the manner of Brahms, are reserved for the last four bars of
the passage), ending with a firm G minor cadence. Very
characteristic of Nielsen is the way he begins his first four
symphonies each with a powerful outburst of the orchestral
tutti. Apart from the clash of the two main tonalities this
opening contains one other point of prime importance; four
bars before letter A it shows signs of settling in E flat, a key that
is equally related to G minor and the Mixolydian C major.
As will be seen, the third movement is in this key. At letter A
itself, however, G minor and the trombones settle the matter

for the moment. The first *piano* brings a subsidiary theme in dialogue between clarinet and bassoon, at first still in G minor; this is developed on its own account and causes a *crescendo* in which there is a shift towards the dominant of B flat, the orthodox 'relative major' of G minor. The new dominant is enforced by another *tutti* at letter B (notice that the young composer is not overscrupulous in his treatment of the timpani; at this point the drum reinforces the basic F with a G, an effect that is in this case justified by the grinding harmony. Often, however, his use of the drums is rather cramped by his refusal to retune them during the course of a movement, so that he can bring them in only when the harmony includes them, even if they are unable to strike the fundamental note. It is illuminating to compare this tentative method with the extraordinary imagination and power with which the timpani are used in the fourth Symphony).

This insistence on the dominant of B flat is suddenly interrupted by a strange B natural (oboes, with bassoons added a beat later). A slight *ritenuto* leads to a new, reflective theme in D flat, of all keys (the B natural was, in reality, a C flat).

Ex. 2

There is some doubt as to whether this is really the right key, and a series of beautiful sequences, in which the flat second in one bar becomes a seventh in the next, brings the music round to C major (page 13, bar 3, *molto tranquillo*). Into this C major creeps the familiar flat seventh, B flat; this time it behaves in the classical manner, leading to F. A new chromatic theme (*agitato*) turns the F quite decidedly into the dominant of B flat and the music is once more on solid ground; there is a swift *crescendo*, a crisp cadence in B flat major, based on the rhythm of Ex. 1(*a*), echoed by bassoons and horns, and the exposition is ended.   A loud chord of G major brings about the repeat by making a perfect cadence with the opening C major chord.   It is vitally necessary to repeat the exposition.

It will at once be noticed that this exposition, though its material may remind one at times of Brahms or Dvořák (with a possible Russian influence—perhaps Borodin—in Ex. 2), has a Scandinavian terseness all its own.   Even though its range of harmony is extremely wide, the variety of its subject-matter great, and the flexibility of its rhythms remarkably free, the sum effect is of a blunt shortness of address, very remote from a romantic manner.   Yet there is no lack of warmth and spontaneity.   It could be by no other composer.   One masterly and genuinely 'Nielsenesque' stroke is his method of preparing B flat: the trenchant dominant preparation at letter B is interrupted, but not effaced, by the apparent modulations that follow it.   These harmonic inflexions take place under the shadow of this preparation, so that when the B flat is finally established it still feels quite firmly grounded.   Later Nielsen was able to increase the scale of this device, as will be shown in the finale of the *Sinfonia espansiva*.

The development begins with a muttering in the rhythm of Ex. 1(*a*) on the dominant of B flat (with the characteristic flat seventh, in this case an A flat).   The clarinet takes up an augmentation of this figure, bassoon and oboe join, and the key becomes a clear F major with the entry of Ex. 2 in the strings. This is taken over by the woodwind and flows along, soon passing through E flat, the dominant of A flat.   In A flat a new phase begins.   Starting *pp* (letter C) Ex. 1(*a*), augmented in *staccato* crotchets, rises sequentially in a *crescendo* very rapidly, landing in D major.   From A flat to D is, tonally, the furthest possible distance, a tritone, and this relationship (or, rather, opposition of poles) becomes increasingly fascinating to Nielsen as he grows older, and is treated with the greatest possible power

in the fifth Symphony. In this case, of course, there is as yet
no far-reaching significance in it: the process starts again in
D major; if it were to remain a strict sequence, it would complete a circle and return to A flat. But at the last moment it
avoids the chromaticism that would bring this about and tilts
the music straight into the key of B minor at letter D. Here a
fiery *tutti*, still based on Ex. 1, begins with what is almost a
foreshadowing of the opening of the *Allegro collerico* in *The
Four Temperaments*, and drives with many disruptions of
rhythm in some unknown direction. At the seventh bar after
letter D, the bass starts to descend by semitones, and in two
bars reaches C (*ff*) as part of a six-four chord of F major. The
descent continues; in another four bars the bass arrives at G,
when the texture changes again. The bass still goes down
chromatically, gets to C sharp, goes up again, and heaves about
before reaching C natural, when it resumes its descent for two
more bars. At letter E it overshoots the note G and falls one
step further to F sharp, by which time the orchestra is ablaze
on the dominant of G. All the while this process has been
been going on, the rest of the orchestra has been boiling up
increasingly furious excitement with transformed fragments of
Ex. 1. When the tension is at its height, the trombones throw
out, in impressive isolation, the crotchet-augmentation of
Ex. 1(*a*), and a moment later the recapitulation crashes into a
G minor that allows no doubts as to its supremacy.

For an early work this development section shows an
astonishing cumulative sense, and, even more than the exposition, shows the hand of the born symphonist. The whole
section is conceived as a single process and the steady increase of
musical and dynamic pressure throughout is felt and contrived
as only a master could do it. For all its feeling of spontaneous
unity, it yet is able to make certain of exploring tonal regions
that the exposition had left untouched, and it succeeds in
creating an inevitable onrush towards G minor (through D

major and B minor) while at the same time hinting at the faint possibility that the key of C might at any time take control.

The restatement commences with Ex. 1, except that the C major chord is now supplanted by a plain G minor one; there is also a crotchet-augmentation of (*a*) on the trombones, and the bass is different. There is not now the long *tutti* that opened the work, since this passage is this time itself the end of a far longer one, and it soon makes a formal close in G minor, two bars after letter F. Now in any ordinary symphony the recapitulation would concern itself with pointing home the re-establishment of the tonic key: but as has already been shown this is no normal sonata movement, and the resumption of G minor is by no means the end of the story. There comes now an expansion for which there are three salient reasons: (1) it is necessary to compensate for the shortening of the opening *tutti*, even though this now has the weight of the development behind it; (2) it is important that G minor should not, at this stage, overload the structure—it must be questioned; (3) Nielsen's plan is so essentially progressive in character that he wants to fuse development and restatement into a continuous process: he holds the view that the device of recapitulation, while it is profoundly necessary to any large structure, must not on any account be allowed to hold up the flow of the main idea. In his early grasp of this principle he shows his deep conviction that in all art the form itself is the expression of the content. In the later works this becomes a much more obvious fact, not because the works themselves are more elaborately wrought, but because the content itself is far more sharply defined.

The *tutti* that falls away at letter F is followed, as before, by the subsidiary idea, slightly altered and without the attendant bassoon figure; its harmony also is changed so that alternate bars contain chords of C major. The harmony deepens into A flat, and the melody spreads into a brief syncopated passage

that seems faintly haunted by the moment in Brahms's D minor
Concerto where the piano makes its own variant of the second
episode theme of the finale. (Another point is the way in
which Nielsen has now altered the 'subsidiary theme' so that
it is now derived from Ex. 1(a): this is merely one sign of his
correct feeling that a real restatement is not a photograph but a
memory, that a good memory always relates facts to experience.)
This little rhythmic tag [from Ex. 1(a)] builds itself into a
crescendo and, by a chromatic movement of the bass, the music
moves towards the dominant of B flat. At letter G the
harmony seems to reject this, there is a sudden interjection of
the note B natural [1] seven bars later (trumpets), and a resultant
turn to the surprising key of E major. This bright key is the
perfect foil to the dark D flat which began the second group in
the exposition, and it is important to remember that in neither
context does D flat or E major behave like a key in its own
right. In E major the oboe picks up Ex. 1(b), the harmony
brightens still more, and Ex. 2 tries to begin in F sharp major;
but there is some hesitation at this, and a last minute harmonic
change brings in the 'second subject' in the grey daylight of
B flat major. The sense of inevitability is, of course, due to the
dominant preparation for B flat just before letter G, and is
another example of a technique that was to become increasingly
meaningful in Nielsen's music. Again, literal repetition will
not do, and he changes the next sequential passage, being
content, after all these events, with a simple succession of
dominant sevenths that take him to the dominant of G.
Notice that whereas the second group originally ended in B
flat, it now opens in that key and veers away from it. B flat
major, like E flat, is a neutral region relative to G minor and
C (in this Mixolydian world).

Unlike the exposition the restatement has no formal close

[1] The selfsame note that previously behaved as C flat just before the entry of
Ex. 2 in D flat.

and the coda begins with an increase of pace to *allegro molto*.
Over a pedal G, the violas give out a new derivative of Ex. 1,
in the manner of a fugue subject: but there are no fugues in this
symphony. Cellos answer a semitone higher (or, rather, a
major seventh lower) in A flat, first violins enter in F minor,
second violins in D minor, all over the pedal G, and the confusion is complete. The *crescendo* that was under way falters
and the bass shifts to C. Is C major going to snatch order out
of chaos? Oboes and bassoons try to insist on G minor (last
bar, page 47 et seq.); they succeed in forcing the bass down to
B flat, then it falls a step more to A flat, which even at this
stage is quite capable of behaving either like a flat supertonic
or a flat sixth in G minor or C major respectively. But the
stern G minor gains the day and whips the music into a last
stretto, where it ends (significantly) with forcible plagal cadences.

From the very first it is a main characteristic of the Nielsen
symphony that its tonal structure extends through the whole
work: he is never content to leave individual movements self-
contained. Thus the struggle between G minor and C major
affects the course of every movement in No. 1. The *Andante*
remains in G throughout its length, turning as if by nature to
the minor for the middle section. There are *inflexions* of other
keys, but no real modulations. The piece is, in fact, a single
enormous melody; its only resting point is its end, and it is
only one of many examples of Nielsen's inborn gift for sustaining the most long-breathed melodic invention without ever
losing his hold on the unity of the full conception. Other fine
pieces of thinking on similar lines are the slow movements of
the A major violin Sonata and the E flat string Quartet, to
mention only early works. To give some idea of the freedom
and economy that inform this movement would mean quoting
it all: it must be enough to indicate its opening phrase, so
poignantly touching, yet so masculine and utterly free from
sentimentality.

Ex. 3

The sudden hardening into bare octaves is very personal to Nielsen; it is his way of repudiating the sentimental half close that would have occurred to most composers in 1892 and, what is of more positive value, his way of insisting on the prime importance of the melodic element.   The continuation brings the first part of the melody to a small climax, and its softly rocking cadence falls into the minor.   This cadence introduces triplet rhythm and the middle section, in G minor, is nearly all in 12–8 time.   It begins with a plaintive oboe figure with a chromatic accompaniment and then rises to a more sus⁄ tained passage (letter B) in which the G minor tends to smile in the direction of B flat major, rather in the manner of Dvořák. Immediately after this comes a phrase that is so typical that it must be quoted:

Ex. 4

C

Superficially one might be reminded of Brahms, but this is one of those passages that in actual performance seem to conjure up the image of Carl Nielsen's very face itself. The expressiveness of the passage is heightened by his penetrating harmonic originality and perfect reserve. This raises the temperature of the music to a big central apex that may remind some hearers of that in the *Adagio* of Brahms's second Symphony. When it dies away, G major returns and the first idea floats in under softly moving triplet quavers in the violins, a moment of real poetry. The octave passage at the end of Ex. 3 is now wreathed in triplet motion; this is clearly derived from Brahms's third, but is none the less individual for that. At the end a short *codetta* is all that is needed to give the movement poise.

The third movement, *Allegro comodo*, is a restrained but purposeful scherzo in E flat. Under a quietly swinging accompaniment a bassoon introduces the phrase marked (*a*) and over it comes the real theme (*b*), cool and clear like the ripple of fresh water.

Ex. 5

Its successive phrases rise sequentially by tones and the ripple becomes a wave that decisively confirms E flat at letter A. But is it really decisive? E flat is a no-man's land between G minor and the C major that has a B-flat in it, and is in this context not likely to be stable. At once comes a new Brahmsish idea in *C minor*, in cross-rhythms:

Ex. 6

A few bars later this brightens hopefully into *C major*; then the tonality becomes disturbed as if a hand were agitating the water from underneath. By letter B, *G minor* has emerged, but it too is unstable and tends to slip into E flat:

Ex. 7

Then the stress grows and the first section of the movement comes to a definite close in E flat major. All this is marked to be repeated and should be heard twice, the more pointedly since Ex. 6 is not heard again in the movement. Next comes an *Andante sostenuto* in G minor that seems at first to be the beginning of a trio; this is not its purpose, however, and it is in fact only a slow version of Ex. 7. It makes a point of emphasizing chords of C major in its fifth, sixth, seventh, ninth, and tenth bars. The last held C major chord causes the clarinet to take up Ex. 5(a) in F major in the original tempo, and it becomes clear that Nielsen is embarking on a kind of development section. Now in a true sonata movement the object of the development is to *lead back* to the original tonic from the key newly established at the end of the exposition. Hence the excellent German term *Durchführung*. Why should a development be needed here if the 'exposition' ended in the tonic, E flat? The reason is this: E flat was not properly established at the end of the exposition (the fact that really makes the repeat psychologically right): C minor-major and G minor saw to that. So a development is not only admissible here, but vital.

The next stage of this development occurs at letter D with a *fortissimo* in C minor, turning abruptly to E flat minor (the notation of this second key is in sharps). Accents in the brass and swirling chromatic scales in the woodwind drive home E flat minor and there is a *diminuendo* on the enhanced home dominant, a chord of F. This soon becomes the normal dominant and the recapitulation flows in happily in E flat major, now more firmly settled. Is it? It begins to follow its normal course, rising by a tone as the first step in its sequence: then anxious questions pervade the air; remote keys are hinted at, and E flat is reinstated again only by a very beautiful turn of harmony. At letter G the recapitulation arrives surprisingly at its formal end, not having mustered enough confidence to recall Ex. 6 or the vigorous version of Ex. 7. But the latter raises its questioning head once more, *Andante sostenuto*, in G minor, with the same strange insistence on the C major chords. C major is, of course, the subdominant major of G minor: the only reply left to the supporters of E flat is to assert *their* sub-dominant, which is A flat. But they lack courage and can produce no more than a lily-livered chord of A flat minor: E flat has no enduring state in the world of this symphony, so it packs its belongings and scurries off in a little coda, *Allegro assai*.

Nielsen did not often write a true scherzo; this movement is a fine example of his special kind of steadily moving intermediate *allegro*. There is not a single piece in Brahms that in any way anticipates it, either in style or in tonal purpose, and it can only be properly understood in the light of the whole symphony. Such a treatment of tonality is utterly individual and the delicate, deeply serious humour behind it matches the kindly

twinkle in the keen pair of eyes that looks out of every photograph of the composer.   One warning is needed: it is a mistake
to treat this piece as if it were a sketch or an anticipation of the
Allegro comodo e flemmatico in the second Symphony.   On
paper it may thus strike the superficial glance, but its style, its
faster *tempo*, and its organization are of a different order.

As if spurred by the suggestion of C major near the end of the
previous movement, the finale breaks out exultantly with a big
chord of C; but, as in the first movement, the main theme twists
itself wilfully into G minor.

The strenuous opening paragraph contains at least two significant details: a momentary drop into E flat minor in bars
13–16, followed immediately by bright chords of C major.
It tails off into an unaggressive close in G minor at letter B.
Next comes a whole series of distinct, short ideas, of which (*a*)
and (*b*) are transitional, while (*c*) and (*d*) belong to the
second group in B flat:

B flat is, as in the first movement, the chosen key for the second group, but it is not established here with any marked enthusiasm, and there is no weighty climax to the exposition, which ends soon after letter F. Again the repeat is essential, if only to show that the opening blaze of C major is for the time being extinguished. The development starts by echoing a two-note figure from the end of the exposition; this figure is joined by a syncopated bass (bassoon). Then, in F, the violins begin a melody which is an ingenious blend of Ex. 9(c) and (d): this is handed over to oboe and bassoon while the fiddles combine with it Ex. 8, in G minor. The repeated-note element begins (as so often with Nielsen) to create action by itself; the tonality goes up further to A flat and then, at letter H, to C major (f, marcato). This is one of the best pieces of writing in Nielsen's first period: the music marches with a long athletic stride; at letter I it breaks into a vivid E major, screws up the tension to A minor and C sharp minor, releases a couple of trenchant outbursts in plain octaves, and launches into a very powerful canon in B major (seven bars after letter K). This discharge of energy spends itself and the orchestra catches its breath on the dominant of D flat. The meaning of this brilliant passage becomes clear as soon as its sequel is related to the end of the whole symphony. The same fragment of thematic material slips in softly in D flat (poco tranquillo). The keys of B and D flat are a semitone on either side of C: like the contradictory keys in the Eroica Symphony they cancel each other out, so that the whole passage (which took its first real impetus from the C major forte at letter H) determinedly thrusts the finale in the direction of C. This is confirmed by the fact that, after some hesitation, a *crescendo* forms on a chord of C major eight bars before letter L. At letter L the chord becomes minor and the recapitulation has begun; the twist into G minor, although it is accomplished in the same way, now has less conviction. There is the same touch of E flat minor and this time the C major chords, even though Nielsen has in no way reinforced them, have more point.

G minor holds its ground for the moment and a new deriva- tive of Ex. 9(*a*) comes in broadly and sequentially on a clarinet (this might easily have occurred in a Borodin symphony). Ex. 9(*a*) itself almost pulls the music back into C (minor), but the second group follows in G minor, growing at the same time more excited and less sure of its footing: G behaves once and for all as the dominant of C, and the tempo quickens to *allegro molto*. The final and inevitable C major ending is so terse that it can hardly be called a coda; it is in fact an enlarge- ment of the second group, from which all its material is drawn. The concentrated brevity of the ending is exhilarating in itself; and it is made thus so that it shall not be too distant from the B major–D flat climax of the development.

Symphony No. 1 shows that Nielsen was already clear as to his real path as a composer, for it displays the principle of progressive tonality: indeed, it might not be going too far to say that it is probably the most highly organized first symphony ever written by a young man of twenty-seven. Besides the subtlety and depth of its construction (in fact, the cause of this), there is, moreover, its spontaneous fire and richness of imagination.

About the time when it was composed, Debussy wrote *L'Après-midi d'un faune* and was beginning to sketch *Pelléas et Mélisande*. Dvořák had not yet finished the 'New World' Symphony, and Mahler had completed Parts II and III of the *Lieder und Gesänge aus der Jugendzeit* (he had finished his first

Symphony four years earlier). Sibelius had written his large choral work *Kullervo* and the first version of *En Saga* and was still seven years away from his first Symphony. Richard Strauss was working on *Guntram* (completed in 1893); among Russian composers, Scriabin wrote his Symphony No. 1, Rachmaninoff his first piano Concerto. Verdi's *Falstaff* was nearing completion (produced 1893). Brahms produced his two famous chamber works for clarinet and strings, and Bruckner was absorbed in the ninth Symphony he was never to finish. In England Sir Frederick Cowen was about to deliver himself of his cantata, *The Water Lily*.

CHAPTER III

THE SECOND SYMPHONY

(*The Four Temperaments*)

1901–2

CARL NIELSEN was not much interested in the Straussian concept of 'programme' music, but this is not to say that he thought music, any more than any other part of life, 'absolute.' Like the honest man he was, he felt that the only thing that could be absolute was total reality. His search for the objective view led him away from himself towards his fellow creatures: as the first Symphony is the expression of personal strength and ability, so the second strikes out on what was to be a life-long adventure—the study of human character. This is the inevitable result of his generosity and is served by an increasingly penetrating intelligence: the scope of this study becomes wider as he gets older. In 1901–2 he was at the stage when human beings as individual types interested him deeply: later, though he never lost his instant sympathy for other people (he was always regarded as a person to whom one could open one's mind), he found out how to see human life as part of an historical, evolutionary process. Some years before writing the second Symphony, he had seen in a country inn in Zealand a series of naïve and rather crude paintings, called 'The Four Temperaments.' Harald Knudsen's translation of Nielsen's own programme-note for this symphony is given at the end of this analysis; it was written in the last year of the composer's life, and is a delightfully picturesque account of the music's origin, expressed in the simple unaffected language for which he was famous.

The first movement, *Allegro collerico*, is in B minor: the tonal

25

design of the whole symphony will appear in the course of analysis and need not be described yet. In this fierce *allegro* there is very little pictorial suggestion (in the literal sense) and the music is meant to convey the Choleric Temperament *in all its moods*. Thus it is not a mere outburst of spleen: Nielsen is far too good an artist not to see that each temperament includes elements of the other three. A predominantly choleric man may have gentle, kindly, lovable, even noble characteristics; these help to make him a whole man, and, in the same way, the corresponding elements in the music help to make it a fine piece of symphonic work by supplying it with tonal and dynamic contrasts, expressive range, and formal spaciousness. The movement starts with an angry thunderclap of a theme:

Ex. 10   **Allegro collerico**

This outburst contains several distinct ideas and propels a *tutti* of thirty-two bars (as compared with the twenty-bar passage in No. 1) to a stormy full close in B minor, two bars after letter B. Observe two points: (1) the momentary accentuation of A major at (c) and (2) the equally marked touch of G major at the *pianissimo* (thirteenth bar). The reaction from all this is a theme with subdued but fitful accents, leading to the following lively phrase on the clarinet:

Ex. 11

Becoming more and more agitated, and passing through the major supertonic, this produces a quick *crescendo*, with a reference to Ex. 10(*d*). There is then a sudden expansion to 3–4 time, and a magnificent irruption of what sounds like righteous indignation, a flaming stream of D major, animated by the leap with which Ex. 11 begins. This D major acts as dominant to G major, the music quietens, and the full nobility of the choleric character is asserted by a finely turned oboe phrase, the start of the second group. Note the characteristic flat seventh, and the quaver leap taken over from Ex. 11:

Ex. 12

p espress.   *f*   etc.

Its lofty sweep (it is immediately sung by the strings) is soon disturbed by stirrings of the impulsive semiquaver figure [Ex. 10(*d*)] and boiling point is again reached at letter D, with loud stabs of the 'fitful' rhythms that preceded Ex. 11. The rhythms become increasingly disruptive, culminating in a furious series of *staccato* chords; there is a silent pause, followed by a huge, full-blooded statement of the 'second subject' to make a trenchant climax to the exposition with richly hued, burning harmonies. It rises to *ffff* before it subsides to a soft close in G major. This exposition is on a larger scale than that in the first movement of No. 1: its rhythmic variety and emotional range are greater, more individual. Its tonal structure is not dissimilar from that in Schubert's unfinished symphony, beginning in B minor and having a second group in G major: whereas Schubert starts recapitulating his second group in D major (which would have been the orthodox key in the exposition), Nielsen, when he comes to it again, keeps it in B minor and major. Schubert, of course, takes advantage of a sombre *tutti* to switch the music back to B major, after some hesitation on the dominant of E minor. But Schubert's movement is fixedly tragic: Nielsen's is extravert, enraged. In comparison with that of the opening movement of the first

Symphony, this exposition shows also a more thorough assimilation of its material; first and second groups are more closely related by the way they share ideas.

The drum incites the basses to ejaculate loudly a rhythm that was left sounding quietly at the end of the exposition, and the development breaks out with disjointed fragments, derived from the quaver figure that accompanied the G major theme. The time reverts to 2–4. Some sharp chords lead to the key of E flat (letter F), but Ex. 11 interrupts with an E natural that turns out to be a seventh in F sharp. In F sharp major Ex. 12 enters, in a new rhythm. Again Ex. 11 contradicts the key, this time with a G natural that behaves as a seventh in A. Ex. 12 starts again in A minor and now modulates to C, from which point there begins a *fugato* based on its last bar (letter G). The irate muttering of this *fugato*, whose entries are far from regular (C, A flat, B, G, E flat minor), is aggravated by a biting rhythmic figure that cuts in upon it more and more insistently. By the time E flat minor is reached (third bar of page 26 in the score), the fugal texture begins to solidify; this is extraordinary orchestration—the double-basses playing together with clarinets and bassoons, cellos and violas crossing each other, first and second violins careering above, and brass and oboes hitting accents and sustaining chords: the effect is of a fast tattering temper. At letter H the music thunders into B flat major; the movement of the strings becomes wilder and the lower brass turns the fugue subject into an impetuous melody; the whole development now takes on shape and direction. Triplet rhythms invade the score, keys come and go, and seven bars after letter I the time again broadens formidably to 3–4. This tide of fury finally bursts over on to the dominant of C, and falls away, apparently exhausted. At letter K, as if in remorse at his anger, the choleric one bethinks himself of his more tender side, and Ex. 12 is heard in C minor: but the time has fallen back into 2–4, and this tune is still bound to its altered version, and is unhappy. It wanders to E flat, starts again (clarinet), and goes from there to B major.

Now here is a subtle point. In the *fugato* that preceded the big storm each entry of the subject began on the dominant note of its key (the first entry, for instance, at letter G, is in the key of C, starting on the dominant G); in the third bar of page 26 another entry of the subject appears to come in, on the note G flat. G flat is, of course, F sharp, and if Nielsen were to let the *fugato* pursue the course it set for itself, he would now allow the subject to sound in C flat (= B), of which G flat (= F sharp) is the dominant. B is the tonic. But the ire is now such that the tonic is overshot, and what might have been a premature recapitulation is turned into the finest passage in the whole movement: instead of C flat comes E flat minor with all the consequences described above. Here is proof indeed that it sometimes pays to lose one's temper!

At letter L the music finds itself at last on the threshold of the tonic, and with the sound of the ground-tone the ground-character reasserts itself. With snorts of rage a fierce *crescendo* blasts in the recapitulation, which begins at letter M. The opening *tutti* follows much the same path as before, except that, under the influence of the development, it substitutes triplet rhythms for Ex. 10(*d*). The 'fitful' passage that succeeds it is now broadened and gives rise to a flowing, restive string passage that takes the place of Ex. 11, which is omitted. Then the main theme of the second group, in 2–4 time, sounds in the tonic minor; it becomes more agitated, for this is not its natural state. It misses its tonal footing, slipping on to the dominant of C (at letter P): an energetic passage, based on Ex. 10(*d*) (notice also the woodwind *arpeggii* drawn from the continuation of the B minor tune), works up towards a climax, and with a thrilling sense of reassurance the great 3–4 passage, like a challenging fanfare, sweeps in on the home dominant. After this the 'second subject,' with all its old breadth, can flow in, receive a new sequel, and build up its strenuous yet dignified climax. Many of the details are altered, and Nielsen is careful to reduce somewhat the force of this climax, for he wants to create a bigger one at no great distance.

The recapitulation dies away in B major; notice the won´ derful effect of the trombone in the last two bars of page 55. Immediately, at letter S, comes one of the most original passages in Nielsen's earlier works, a truly ferocious effect: harsh dis´ sonances, roughly scored, with snapping, irregular accents in the strings, set the whole orchestra aflame. At this, Ex. 10(d) rushes precipitately upwards into a *fortissimo* statement of Ex. 10(c), which spreads out into a fine frenzy of extended melody that forces home B minor four bars after letter T. Here the tempo is hastened, and Ex. 10(b), inflated with splendid choler, roars in a final rampage with Ex. 10(d). The actual end is a breath´taking seven bars that are not only rhythmically exciting; they are also masterly harmony.

There remain two small points to mention: the touches of A major and G major near the beginning (seven and three bars respectively before letter A). These serve to hint, in turn, at the end of the whole symphony and at the key of the second group of the first movement and of the whole second movement. This, it will be remembered, is a similar device to that used in the first Symphony, and it becomes increasingly characteristic that the opening of a Nielsen work gives a clue to its subsequent development: the same thing occurs, in fact, in all six sym´ phonies, with increasing subtlety and poetry.

The opening movement of No. 2 is in every respect an advance on that of the G minor Symphony: while the influence of Brahms and Dvořák may still be felt, this in no way impedes the growth of Nielsen's own style. Themes, harmony, orchestration, rhythmic boldness, all these are more sharply defined and enriched: the form is more massive and executed with more confidence. There can be no doubt that this progress is as much the result of his outward-looking mind as of a mere technical development. In the second movement, for instance, the technique is less elaborate than in the *Allegro comodo* of No. 1, but there can be no doubt that the music is expressive of a more sensitive, receptive awareness. To Carl Nielsen the phlegmatic mentality is far from dull, as can be discerned not only from the music itself but also from his very evocative verbal description of the kind of youth the music reflects. The movement takes the shape of a leisurely waltz in G major: the next quotation shows the first phrase of the charming tune, but not the deep harmonic colour that falls across it immediately afterwards. Nor does it show the fact (which should be carefully noted) that the theme is ushered in by a gentle descending figure on the second violins, starting from the note G, which is the flat sixth of the key of the previous movement, B minor.

Ex. 13

The unruffled mood of the music is not disturbed but simply brought to life by the exquisite momentary gleams of other keys that pass across its face, just as the calmest of human counten-ances may be softly lit by a quiet flow of gently joyful feelings. A tiny example of Nielsen's individuality can be found in the return to G major in the bar before letter A; look at the crossing of the first and second violin parts and the way in which the entry of the horn not only adds a warm new colour but also clarifies what might otherwise have been a confused effect. One is reminded of Tovey's famous and amusing (but not altogether convincing) question and answer:

Q. *What is it which we all wish to learn from the Great Masters, and why can we never learn it?*

A. *How to get out of a hole: because they never get into one.*

Holes are all very well, provided they are dug and not fallen into, as all the Great Masters prove to the discomfiture of their imitators. But the phlegmatic person does not much mind even falling into a hole, and not the least phlegmatic aspect of this movement is the way it makes its first modulation to the subdominant at letter B. Now this is the very incarnation of inaction; it is only part of a large process in which the temperament is thoroughly searched. The tune floats in again in C major, the subdominant, and as the thoughts drift amiably by the tonality sinks into a still browner study, so that by letter C they contemplate the port-wine quality of A flat major. In this key the music goes into what suggests a delectable, themeless (not dreamless) sleep, for all the world like some wholly admirable cow chewing the most deliciously unnoticeable cud. This analogy gives no idea of the pastoral beauty of this quietly humorous passage, which is not quite themeless; a charmingly monotonous figure of repeated notes followed by a lazy falling trill hangs about in the air, and key becomes a matter of indifference. At letter D the music reaches G major again, and the bassoons, dimly aware that this is the tonic, and feeling vaguely that something ought to be done about it, begin an unhurried canon, hinting at the descending figure that introduced the first theme at the very beginning. Clarinets join, but they lose sight of the key; the cud-chewing continues, when there is a sudden shock which is, for the information of the more voraciously analytical readers, on the dominant of E flat (this is the barrel falling into the water; see the composer's note). For the moment the atmosphere is disturbed (letter E) but after some delay, the first theme sails in with complete nonchalance in E flat, as if to say 'I'm not in the least surprised —this key will do as well as any other.' The scoring here is beautifully, richly comfortable. The continuation leads to D major (it is typically phlegmatic to relax at such a moment into a lower key), *which is the home dominant.*

D

Now all students of sonata form know about the indolent composer who begins his recapitulation in the subdominant, so that his second group (which originally came in the dominant) will now fall automatically into the tonic, and so save him the trouble of rewriting his transition. All he needs to do is transpose his entire exposition note for note, a mere matter for a copyist. Being a musician himself, Nielsen naturally illustrates the phlegmatic disposition in composers, by going one stage further: since his first section made its first change to the subdominant, and he now dis-covers himself in the dominant, he need only leave the music alone and it will automatically find its way to the tonic. This is what he does; when the tune appears in the tonic it is given a new and engaging twist of the tail; then the whole movement drifts off.

It should now be clear how erroneous it would be to suggest that this piece has much in common with the third movement of the first Symphony, and it is especially unfair to the earlier movement to suppose that it is in any way a preparation for this. Both are unique and each serves its special purpose. As always, Nielsen uses tonality as his chief asset, though this does not obscure the charm and distinction of his melody.

Between the keys of the first and second movements is the interval of a major third, B dropping to G; another major third separates the Phlegmatic from the Melancholic Temperament, which gives vent to its sadness in E flat minor. Also worth noting is the fact that both the middle movements start with a descending figure; in the first case the first note (G) is the flat sixth of the key of the previous movement; in the case of the slow movement the first note is the flat sixth of the new key and the major third of the old. (C flat = B). The themes of the two movements are, moreover, related: here is the start of the long melancholy tune:

Andante malincolico. [1]

Ex. 14

The Melancholic Temperament is not merely helplessly gloomy; its sadness is the result of courageous thought. It is capable of heroism and strong decisions; if it is disillusioned, that is better than being illusioned, any self-pity is rigorously excluded, as is also weak sentimentality. Optimism is sought after, but not often reached. Inevitably, this is the deepest part of the symphony. As the Phlegmatic Temperament began by sinking into the subdominant, so the Melancholic aspires towards the dominant, which marks a firm half-close at letter A. The major chord of B flat turns to G minor, and an oboe laments with a phrase that tends to haunt the ear long after the performance is over:

Ex. 15

This thought is to become even more important than the main theme itself, and it never remains exactly the same. It is taken up by other instruments, over shifting chromatic harmonies and a vast paragraph slowly grows, filled with intensest poignancy; the harmonic freedom and tonal steadiness of this passage rivals anything in Reger, and it is completely free from Reger's tendency to luxuriate (Reger's 'modulations' are, as Harold Truscott once pointed out in a letter to the *Musical Times*, often not modulations at all; they are simply the harnessing

---

[1] It should, of course, be *malinconico*. Nielsen has spelt it wrongly.

of a number of remote keys to a single basic tonality, like satellites round a planet). This great sentence appears to move from key to key, but in reality it never leaves its roots in E flat: when the tonic cadence is heard again it sounds as secure as if the intervening harmony had been the plainest. Notice the majestic effect of Ex. 15 at letter C, as it enters *fortissimo* low down on the heavy brass, without the slightest suggestion of crudeness; although the harmony is continuously chromatic, its basis remains diatonic, and the sound is always firm and clean, utterly unsentimental. The mood of this music is strongly anticipated in the slow movement of the E flat string Quartet, written three years earlier, though the quartet movement makes a point of its active middle section; in the present piece the middle part is static and still founded in E flat. Nielsen's own description again gives the vital pointer to the meaning of this central passage. Its own lack of movement entangles it, as if in a net.

There is no need to quote the material on which this section is based; it is smooth-flowing, treated contrapuntally, with frequent use of a dropping fourth (sometimes extended to a fifth or shortened to a third). English listeners may be tempted to compare this almost motionless music with that by which Elgar describes the disembodied soul's condition at the opening of the second part of *The Dream of Gerontius*: nothing could be more profitable, for the comparison shows instantly the difference between Elgar, the dreamy, religious romantic, and Nielsen, the blunt, logical man of the soil, with both feet on the ground. Elgar regards this static condition as the prelude to a desirable, ecstatic transfiguration: Nielsen sees it as a dangerous state, causing impotence and a return to melancholy. This part of the movement begins on page 93 of the score, with a slight increase of the *tempo*. The orchestral colouring alternates between wind and strings. At letter E a long imitative episode, beginning on the flat supertonic, occupies the woodwind;

this is the passage likened by the composer to the meshes of a net. At letter F the counterpoint is at its most involved, as if struggling with itself: the strings hold the home dominant on a long shake, and there is no escape. The tone subsides until only the soft throb of a drum can be heard. The first theme breaks in with redoubled intensity, the rhythm that was originally on the timpani (see bars 3 and 4) being now made to support the harmony. It moves as before to its dominant half-close and is followed by Ex. 15, at first over a tonic chord. The harmony again takes a winding path, but a totally different one from before: one remarkable moment is at letter H, where there commences a series of entries of Ex. 15, rising by tones, successively taking as points of departure the notes D, E, F sharp, G sharp. This makes a gathering sound of the utmost dolefulness, the more so since Nielsen accepts the full conse-quences of all the clashes of the parts: at a time when many of his colleagues were self-consciously striving to avoid the responsibilities of handling large-scale tonality, or merely reproducing old, worn devices, he created new and startling sounds from his awareness of all the old, traditional principles. These harmonic collisions are so telling because they are felt naturally within the scope of classical tonality. Later, when he was asked his opinion of the so-called 'atonalists,' he remarked that if one took all the colours of the spectrum and dappled them on a disk, the result of rotating the disk would be (most likely) a dirty grey. To him, keys are as inescapable as colours, and must be mastered. If one were to criticize his analogy by saying that the composers he meant do not mix up all the keys, he would no doubt have replied by saying that dirty grey is, in fact, dirty grey.

The result of this passage is a grim but noble outburst on a chord of D minor, another a tone lower on a C major chord, some great detached harmonies, heavily accented, on the full orchestra, and then the last phrase of the whole paragraph in an

E flat minor that has never been shaken. It dies away into a quiet, deeply moving coda which, instead of closing in E flat minor, hovers at last on the brighter dominant major chord of B flat. One is tempted to regard this movement as the highest achievement in Nielsen's first period: noble and grand as is much of *Saul and David*, it contains nothing that matches the musical sustaining power in this *andante*; nor is there anything quite comparable in the *Hymnus amoris*, for all its striking beauty. It far surpasses the slow movement of the first Symphony, both in scale and in depth.

Consider, for a moment, the tonal structure of this work as it has revealed itself so far. Brahms's C minor Symphony (No. 1) is planned with the keys of its movements rising by major thirds; C minor, E major, A flat, and finally C major. The first three movements of Nielsen's second seem to suggest a similar idea, but in the reverse direction, with descending thirds; B minor, G major, E flat minor. Now it would be perfectly straightforward and easy for the poor critic if Nielsen were to follow the rules and put his finale, like a good fellow, in B major. But he has been going down all the time; one certainly can descend from the Choleric to the Phlegmatic, and from there to the Melancholic: but how on earth can one descend another major third from the Melancholic to the Sanguine? Obviously only a philosopher could steer round this argument and still justify B major as the key for the finale. But Nielsen is an artist, and artists (especially musicians) are notoriously lacking in profundity as compared with philo⁄sophers, and are reluctant to sink so low. And so are persons of the Sanguine Temperament. Clearly, this last movement must be in a brilliant key; in this context B major would not be brilliant, for it would not be B major at all; it would be C flat, the warm, dark relative of E flat minor. But D major is a near cousin to B minor, after all, and if sanguine people are frustrated they may easily become choleric, so the finale feels no embarrassment at all in springing out gaily in D major, which is like a burst of sunlight after the subdued chords of B flat that ended the slow movement.

Ex. 16

Allegro sanguineo.

(♩ = 132)

ff

fz

fz

etc.

The Sanguine man cares not a fig for the world; difficulties do not deter him, for he has never heard of difficulties; he is full of rude vigour and gusty laughter.   There have been very few genuine expressions of the Sanguine in music since Beethoven's 'unbuttoned' mood.   Perhaps Berlioz, in *Le Corsaire* overture, comes very near to it: the finale of Schubert's great C major Symphony has too much solemnity behind it, and Brahms certainly never approached it.   Richard Strauss often makes bluff, full-blooded effects, but underneath them all is the indolence of the predominantly sensual man: Mahler occasion-ally tries but is too nervous.   Most twentieth-century com-posers are much too self-conscious to write sanguine music. Of the older British composers Elgar is too circumstantial and Vaughan Williams too innately reflective, and it would be fair to say, perhaps, that the British are not a very sanguine group of races.   The precise character of Beethoven's 'unbuttoned' movements (the ending movements of the seventh and eighth Symphonies, for instance) is still practically unique.   This finale certainly does not compare with Beethoven's in point of structural strength or subtlety of organization, and it is perhaps the more truly sanguine for that.   But it does throw off a remarkably similar kind of abandon; the kind for which Beethoven was condemned by those of his contemporaries who found it naïve and preposterously noisy. For all its simplicity, however, there are real subtleties in this movement: Nielsen's Sanguine character cares so little about the fact that, in his opening career, he has ridden roughshod over the key of B flat (the dominant of the Melancholic), that he bolts straight from there into A major (his own dominant) with a thunderous shouting of his own tune (at letter B). The music tears headlong, apparently careless of the territories of its tonal neighbours, the violins keeping up a furious stream of rushing quavers and the brass and bass instruments galumphing hugely up and down in massive scales. Soon after letter D, the exultant tumult is checked by harsh intrusions and after a series of tremendous syncopations, it dies out in some bewilderment. Again Nielsen is too good an artist to believe in a theoretical human being: not even the most sanguine person who ever lived was completely unaware of conflicts, and the result here is that the second subject, jaunty as it is, wears a slightly worried look:

Ex. 17

It is in the orthodox dominant, A, but minor, and it gradually shakes off its doubts, becoming more and more energetic (the passage at letter G is, besides being quietly vigorous, harmonically very beautiful, and it leads to eight bars in A flat that remind one so irresistibly of Dvořák that one wonders if that composer might have written some genuine sanguine music: indeed, he might have done so were it not for the ease with which he slips into melancholy). A *crescendo* brings about a very loud, happy, and selfsatisfied climax in A major. It dies away slowly, with a suggestion of the main theme from flute and another from second violins, and appears content: but the drum wakes it up again and the recapitulation is in full swing.   There is not even a suspicion of a develop‑ ment section; that would be quite wrong here.   The theme follows the same rough road as before, passing through B flat before crashing into A major: then, at the second bar of page 141, the music takes a new turn, stampeding heedlessly on to a *fff* chord of the subdominant, G major, at letter O.

Now there are many things that the Sanguine Temperament cannot possibly grasp.   Among these is undoubtedly the fact that this rich, sumptuous subdominant chord of G major can, if it likes, behave as the dominant of the dark, mysterious C minor.   It is, of course, time to restate the second subject: this was a trifle disturbed when it first appeared, but that was nothing compared with its dismay as it now gropes its way painfully, *Adagio molto,* through the labyrinthine mists and murks of this unknown region, C minor.   At one moment the light seems to glow faintly, but the groping peters to a stand‑ still: then there is a real gleam, a soft *tremolando* chord of C major.   It brightens, there is a *crescendo,* the bass finds its way downwards with increasing confidence, and the upper instru‑ ments begin to feel the approach of the main tune.   To every‑ one's surprise (and to all the intellectuals' embarrassment) the full orchestra bursts out with the tune, transformed into a rousing A major march, and the symphony is over.   Any one who finds this ending too 'simple' or 'naïve' had better examine carefully its immensely powerful and original bass, though a listener who has to go thus far before seeing the point is likely to miss many of the simpler and completer joys of life.   Another thing about this ending is that it is in the key that is not only the dominant of the movement's D major, but is also the major flat seventh in relation to the first movement's B minor.   What could be more sanguine than that?   It will be remembered, too, that A major was the first tendency of the *Allegro collerico.*

Contemporary with the second Symphony were the following works by other composers: Delius, *A Village Romeo and Juliet*; Fauré, *Pelléas et Mélisande*; Mahler, Symphony No. 4; Sibelius, Symphony No. 2; Elgar, *The Dream of Gerontius* (completed 1900); Strauss, *Feuersnot*; Ravel, *Jeux d'eau*; Stanford, *Much Ado about Nothing*; Rimsky-Korsakov, *Servilia*; Rachmaninoff, second piano Concerto; Saint-Saëns, *Les Barbares*; Debussy, *Nocturnes* completed; Holst, *The Youth's Choice* (unpublished opera); Reger, Sonata in C, Op. 72 (violin and pianoforte), Variations on an Original Theme, Op. 73 (organ), String Quartet No. 3 in D minor, Op. 74.

CARL NIELSEN'S NOTE ON 'THE FOUR TEMPERAMENTS'

I

The notion for the symphony *The Four Temperaments* came to me years ago in a village pub in Zealand. In the saloon where I was having some beer with my wife and some friends, there hung a most comical picture. It was in four parts, which showed the temperaments with the titles: *The Choleric, The Phlegmatic, The Melancholic,* and *The Sanguine.* The choleric man was on horseback; he had a long sword in his hand, with which he slashed wildly at the empty air, his eyes were nearly rolling out of his head, his hair flew madly round his face; it was so full of fury and devilish hate that involuntarily I burst into laughter. The other three pictures were in the same style and my friends and I were highly amused at their naïvety and their exaggerated expressions and comical gravity. But how oddly things turn out! I, who had laughed loudly and derisively at these pictures, found my thoughts constantly returning to them, and one fine day it was clear to me that these simple paintings contained a core of goodness and—even—a musical possibility into the bargain. Later on I began to work out the first movement of the symphony, but I had to be careful that it didn't hit into the empty air and hoped, of course, that my listeners wouldn't laugh and that the tables wouldn't be turned on me. I tried to turn the pictures into another idea, and now I will give a modest account of my Symphony No. 2, *The Four*

Temperaments. The first movement, *Allegro collerico,* starts impetuously with a theme that develops with another little theme on the clarinet and rises to a fanfare leading to the second subject, which sings very *espressivo,* but is soon interrupted again by violently shifting figures and rhythmic jerks. After a pause, the second subject, *ff,* unfolds itself with greater breadth and strength, which gradually pass away, when the development begins; here the above-mentioned material is worked, now wildly and impetuously, like one who nearly forgets himself, now in softer mood, like one who regrets his irascibility. Lastly comes a coda (*stretto*) with vehement passages in the strings, and the movement ends in the same temper as it started.

II

The second movement is meant to be a complete contrast to the first. I don't like programme music, but perhaps it may interest my listeners to know that during the preparatory work I thought of something like the following: I visualized a young fellow. He was his mother's only son. The mother was sweet and amiable, a widow, and was very fond of him. He also was uncommonly lovable, and everybody was attached to him. He was about 17–18 years old, with sky-blue eyes, confident and big. In school he was loved by all, but the teachers were at the same time in despair and, in a mild way, gave him up; for he never knew his lessons. But it was impossible to scold him, for everything idyllic and heavenly in nature was to be found in this young lad, so that every one was disarmed. Was he jolly or serious, was he lively or slow in his movements? None of these things! His real inclination was to lie where the birds sing, where the fish glide noiselessly through the water, where the sun warms and the wind strokes mildly round one's curls. He was fair; his expression was rather happy, but not self-complacent, rather with a hint of quiet melancholy, so that one felt impelled to be good to him. When the air was shimmering in the heat, he would usually be lying on the pier at the harbour, with his legs dangling over the edge. I have never seen him dance; he wasn't active enough for that, though he might easily have got the idea to swing himself in a gentle slow waltz rhythm, so I have used that for the movement, *Allegro comodo e flemmatico,* and tried to stick to one mood, as far away as possible from energy, emotionalism,[1] and such things. Only once is there a *forte.* What's that? Did a barrel fall into the harbour from a ship, disturbing the young chap lying

---

[1] Nielsen quotes the German word 'Gefühl.'

on the pier dreaming? Maybe. So what? In a moment everything
is quiet again: the lad falls asleep, the world dozes, and the water is again
smooth as a mirror.

III

The third movement tries to express the basic character of a heavy,
melancholy man, but here as always in the domain of music, the title or
programme is only a pointer. What the composer himself wants has
less significance than what the music's innermost essence is searching for.
After a bar and a half of introduction, the theme begins, drawn heavily
towards a strong outcry of pain (ff); then comes, on the oboe, a little
plaintive sighing motive, that slowly develops, ending in a climax of
lamentation and suffering. After a short transition there is a quieter,
resigned episode in E flat major. A long, somewhat static passage now
follows, at the end of which the parts intertwine like the threads of a net,
and everything subsides; then suddenly the first theme breaks out with
full force, the various motives sing together, and the whole moves to its
close, where it sinks to rest.

IV

In the finale, *Allegro sanguineo*, I have tried to sketch a man who storms
thoughtlessly forward in the belief that the whole world belongs to him,
that fried pigeons will fly into his mouth without work or bother. There
is, though, a moment in which something scares him, and he gasps all at
once for breath in rough syncopations: but this is soon forgotten, and even
if the music turns to minor, his cheery, rather superficial nature still asserts
itself.

All the same there is, just for once, a time when it seems as if he has met
with something really serious; at least he cogitates about something or
other that seems foreign to his character, and it seems to influence him this
much, that the final march, though joyous and bright, is yet more dignified and not so silly and self-satisfied as in some of the previous parts of his
development.

Copenhagen, 1st Sept. 1931.   *Carl Nielsen.*

CHAPTER IV

THE THIRD SYMPHONY

(*Sinfonia espansiva*)

1910–11

THE period before the First World War found Nielsen at the height of his musical powers and the two main works of the years 1910–11, the *Sinfonia espansiva* and the violin Concerto, express to the full that warm and sunny aspect of him that has led to the popular over-simplification of the comparison between him and Sibelius: the Finn is said to be 'grim' and the Dane 'genial.' As in all popular generalizations, there is some truth in this; Nielsen's personality is far more approach-able than Sibelius's, but the Danish composer's fifth and sixth Symphonies and his clarinet Concerto are in some ways tougher in fibre even than such a work as the concentrated fourth Symphony of Sibelius. It is undoubtedly the popu-larity of *The Four Temperaments*, and perhaps to a slightly greater extent the *Espansiva*, that has given rise to the impression that Nielsen's music is always smiling. In relation to the rest of Scandinavia, the Danish atmosphere might almost be called Mediterranean, and the third Symphony completely sums up this attractive side of the country and its generous, hospitable people. Besides this, the work has an enormous vigour and its title betokens the composer's now full consciousness of his own powers; he feels now not only a keen interest in the tempera-ments and characters of his fellows; he understands that this is not a mere feeling of sympathy, but one of actual identity of purpose. He realizes what he at first only sensed, that he and his music are dependent on and of value to the ordinary, straightforward folk among whom he feels at home. The result is that the personal strength on which he relied in the works of his first period is matured, canalized, and redoubled by a very real feeling of solidarity with the people. Thus *espansiva* means the outward growth of the mind's scope and the expansion of life that comes from it. It has no 'romantic' connotations, and does not mean inflation; the symphony is scarcely longer than No. 2, and its title, like all good titles, simply confirms what the work says in its own clear terms. Why, then, bother with a title? Because an artist who has something precise to say will say it in terms of his art, but, if he is not afraid to do so, may also seize any other means of communication (of which language is the most generally used), to make sure that his audience, viewers, or readers will be prepared for it.

This symphony carries further Nielsen's mastery of tonality as the basis of structure. The expansive nature of the thought is illustrated by three characteristics, all interlinked in a continuous process which, as usual, braces the whole work. First, the symphony progresses from D minor to its dominant major, A major. Second, there is (particularly in the first two movements) a strong tendency to form rising 'terraces' of keys; from Fig. 2 onwards in the first movement, for instance, the successive keys are F sharp minor (preceded by the dominant of F), G minor, G sharp minor (then *almost* A, some inflexions of other keys, and, at Fig. 6, A flat = G sharp), B flat minor (Fig. 9), C major (Fig. 11): this process will be analysed in due course. Third, there is a frequent tendency to move to the remotest possible distance from a given key: the powerful opening paragraph, for instance, swings half way round the universe from D minor to A flat minor-major. This last very expansive urge is also at the centre of the symphony, the heart of the slow movement, a famous passage in E flat, the remotest possible key from the final destination A. But this is to anticipate academically what is, in truth, an experience that will be made sharper by a point-to-point analysis.

Like the first two symphonies, No. 3 opens with a flood of full orchestral tone; as compared with the 20 bars of *tutti* in No. 1 and the 32 bars in No. 2, the *Espansiva* starts its career with a vast sweep of 137 bars (including the final 20 bars of *diminuendo* before the second group). These are, it is true, shorter bars, but even so, the length of this paragraph is more than twice that of its predecessor. This first movement, *Allegro espansivo*, is the first great example of Nielsen's character-istic and exhilarating 3-4 movements, whose muscular swinging stride is first foreshadowed in the finale of the A major violin Sonata, Op. 9 and more restrainedly followed up by the first movement of the F major string Quartet of 1906 (Op. 44). (The third movement of the first Symphony and the *flem-matico* in No. 2 are cases apart.)   Here is Carl Nielsen the fit, open-air countryman, in the finest condition, both mental and physical.   The actual start is a series of huge hammer-blows, rapidly accelerated into a tattoo; the accents are irregular, on the note A, and the ear does not catch the fundamental 3-4 pulse until the following theme flies, as it were, off the anvil in D minor:

This opening *tutti,* as already noted, drives from D minor to the most distant key, A flat, and it does so in the following manner. Remember that the eventual goal of the entire symphony is A *natural* major; this means that the opening attack

is a determined attempt to reach this key, falling short at A flat.
There is internal evidence to support this idea. First the note
A is thrust out as a proposition, but it leads to D minor;
immediately, the music tries to reach F major (half way
between D and A), for which it makes vehement dominant
preparation six bars before Fig. 2. Impetuously it overshoots
the mark into F sharp minor (at Fig. 2 itself) with a derivative
of Ex. 18(c): eight bars later the tonality screws itself up another
semitone into G minor with another, extended statement of the
main subject (almost every time this tune appears it becomes a
new tune, usually by expansion). Then at Fig. 3 it rises with
an even severer sense of effort to G sharp minor, continuing
with wide-sweeping melody. Only one more step will reach
A. That step is attempted valiantly at Fig. 4; a chord of A
minor is actually reached (*fff*), but it falls away into C minor,
which turns to C major with a figure that has evolved out of the
extension of the main theme:

Ex. 19

The stepwise progression of keys is now momentarily broken,
and C major behaves as dominant of F (the key that was overshot earlier); in F major comes a powerful canonic treatment of
Ex. 19(a) on trumpets and trombones. This F is the half-way
house that was missed at Fig. 1; perhaps there is now hope of
reaching A? A new effort is made, but the interruption was
too strong; the music succeeds in rising out of F, but reaches
only A flat minor (= the previous G sharp minor), still a
semitone short of its goal. Just before Fig. 6, trombones and
bassoons thunder out the main subject in A flat minor; the
high point of tension is reached at Fig. 6 itself (*ffff*) and the

Carl Nielsen's Study

climax flares out with considerable grandeur on the dominant
of A flat. Notice how the trombones make a very impressive
break in the first note of Ex. 18(*b*), leading into a suggestion of
the opening rhythm, which this time spends itself instead of
gathering momentum.

All this high discharge of power makes certain, for the time
being, that A flat shall be established, and it is in this key that
the second group opens with the following contrasting idea.
It contains references to Ex. 18(*b*) and (*c*):

Ex. 20

Molto tranquillo   18 (c)   18 (b)

FLUTE *mp*

CLARINETS *p*

After a calm continuation and a muttering interjection from
the strings, this is counterstated in the local subdominant, thus
disturbing any immediate prospects that this A flat might still
become A natural.   The rising trend, however, continues, but
this time the key moves up a whole tone to B flat minor,
missing out A.   A new, soft-flowing theme is heard (Fig. 9).

Ex. 21

1st VIOLINS

etc.

p

At Fig. 10 waltz rhythms begin to dance in; then comes a
pianissimo fugato, light as thistledown, all on the dominant of
B flat. Suddenly an imperious *fortissimo* breaks out with
rushing quavers in the strings and whips the tonality up
another tone to C major (Fig. 11).   In C major Ex. 20 sails
out grandly, and is broadened into a fine sentence with great
descending phrases that recall Ex. 19 and its origins.   This is a
large *tutti* passage, and it ends the exposition firmly in C major,

E

dying away very effectively with strong *pizzicato* chords bound together by sustained clarinets.   It is important to remember this big C major passage; it succeeds for the first time in fixing a key with an unmistakable full close; later, Nielsen summons it for a similar purpose.   (The fixing of A flat after Fig. 6 has not the same air of finality.)

In analysing this remarkable movement the use of normal sonata terminology can be misleading; the music evolves steadily from the beginning to the end, whereas the tonal development of a normal sonata movement takes place in clearly separable stages, even in the more complex of Schubert's or Reger's compositions.   This *Allegro espansivo* is a tonal forge; everything is as fluid as molten metal, out of which something is to be made: unlike most sonata movements, this is a form only in so far as one can find in it a process from which the rest of the symphony is enabled to emerge.

The influence of C major hangs over the next forty-three bars; the 'development' starts with a new and graceful waltz-like figure on the dominant of A minor (which is closely related to C major); the quaver figure is cunningly derived from Ex. 18:

Ex. 22

Ex. 18(*a*) enters canonically in A minor, between cellos and second fiddles: the waltz figure chips in again and C major returns at Fig. 15, with the same kind of canon between horn and bassoon.   Then there is an abrupt modulation to G sharp minor and Ex. 18(*a*) is transformed into an exquisite waltz. A significant feature of this engaging idea, which begins at Fig. 15, is its immediate waft to the opposite pole, D major. The D major slides on to the dominant of F sharp (Ex. 22 on lower strings, four bars before Fig. 16), and then Ex. 18(*a*), combined with Ex. 22, comes out in F sharp minor. Notice the cunning shift of accents in the second phrase, in which the minor becomes major. The atmosphere becomes gayer as a pattering *fugato* (based on the end of the new waltz-transformation of Ex. 18) swings from key to key, settling in an exuberant *crescendo* on the dominant of B flat: the *crescendo* becomes enormous and lasts sixteen bars, with immense dominant fundaments shaking the depths; the waltz has no choice but to swing out tumultuously in B flat minor. As before, it swoops at once to the opposite pole, in this E major (Fig. 18 et seq.). With bounding vim the melody grows and expands until the whole world seems to be singing and dancing: before long all the strings (except the impervious double-basses), two trumpets, and the bassoons are sustaining a sweeping *cantabile* in F sharp minor. It comes to a grand climax twelve bars before Fig. 19 on (scarcely *in*) its dominant minor, C sharp minor; a mysterious *diminuendo* then leaves only one viola and one cello remembering what has happened. The 'development' is over.

In more than one sense it is a real development: the thematic material continually grows into new shapes, the whole is in effect a long *crescendo*, and it gravitates tonally from the region of C major to the region of F sharp (another opposition of poles). This section cannot be said to serve the same function as its more usual counterpart (i.e. to lead back from the exposition's new-key ending to the home tonic; so far in this movement no home tonic has been decisively fixed, for it is in process of being evolved), but there is a clear difference between its behaviour and that of the exposition. In the exposition the keys follow a scheme (rising by steps) which, once it has been observed, is as direct as the old tonic-to-dominant trend of the classical exposition: this development is, like the old sonata *Durch-führung*, much freer in its wanderings from key to key, and is unified by its start and finish in specially selected keys. Perhaps it should be emphasized that these matters are not in the least 'technical'; they are artistic facts that are at the root of the music's expressive content.

The third and last part of the movement may be called a blend of recapitulation and coda. The trailing viola and cello seem undecided whether to stick to C sharp or to go back to F sharp, and instead of either, slip to F: Ex. 18(*a*) drifts quietly in on a flute in F minor. There is still more indecision about the key; D minor is tried, C major, A major, E minor: horns enter eight bars after Fig. 20 and cause a superb modulation to E flat. In E flat the second group begins to recapitulate itself. Where is the first? Wait and see. As before, Ex. 20 is counterstated in the local subdominant (A flat in this case) and is followed by Ex. 21 in the key a tone higher than at the start of the group: before it was B flat minor, now it is in F minor (Fig. 23). Last time, B flat minor was followed by the *tutti* outburst in C major, still a tone higher: this time, after passing through the same waltz rhythms and the whispering *fugato* (slightly changed in details), no one would be surprised to hear the *tutti* break out in G major, one tone above F minor. What actually occurs is the crucial incident of the movement. The *tutti* does crash in, but in A major! (Fig. 25.)

Now it becomes clear why Nielsen was at such pains to base his exposition on a long stepwise 'terrace' of keys: there is no better way of ramming a point well and truly home than to create a habit of mind and then deliberately cut across it. Even though the vast majority of listeners would have no conscious idea of the systematic process that has been going on (any more than they are conscious of their own breathing), their previous hearing of this passage makes this restatement of it familiar. Its familiarity breeds not contempt but the enjoyment of recognition. Thus the jolt of the substitution of A major for G major with this powerful burst of the full orchestra makes its mark even on those who do not understand why the effect sounds rather more brilliant than it did before. Add to this the fact that the original C major climax was associated with the only really satisfying full close in the whole piece, and the full genius of Nielsen's device is revealed. A major is now, at a stroke, wedded to the idea of a full close: a step forward indeed. The symphony is surely finding its direction.

Naturally such a device has not the obvious force of domi⸍nant preparation; this is as it should be, for the first movement by no means clinches the matter. What follows now is in the nature of a restatement of most of the great opening sweep, with the inevitable expansions, in which all the remaining threads are powerfully knotted into a sinewy whole. A major at this stage is still not free from the urge to turn dominant to D minor: at Fig. 26 it does so, invoking a massive D minor canon on Ex. 18(a), with Ex. 20 weighing in upon it after a few bars. At Fig. 27, fierce detached chords protest (recalling the rhythm of the very opening), and six bars after Fig. 28, A major is strenuously restored with the entry of Ex. 19. Again its grip loosens as it goes this time to D major with the quasi⸍canon that followed Ex. 19 in the exposition. Still the tension mounts, as D major becomes minor at Fig. 30, where Ex. 18(a) expands into pounding crotchets. Suddenly the air is charged with mystery and the volume drops to *ppp*. Soft brass change the previous pounding into a faint pulse, and woodwind turn Ex. 18(b) into an expressionless intoning in a strange C sharp minor; *pizzicato* strings touch off from time to time the quavers of (c). The key shifts in the queerest and most impressive manner, there is a *crescendo* and at Fig. 32 a return to *forte*, but in F major. Where is he going? But he is right; such a stroke as this is the only answer to the influence of D minor. C sharp and F are each a major third away from A, above and below; they are, in this context, 'contradictory' keys, each annihilating the other. So A major can now take possession at Fig. 33; not having adequate dominant preparation, it is still not quite happy, and falls to A minor in seven bars. One final surge of effort, and the movement ends with a bright chord of A major. Enough has been accomplished to settle the destination of the work, and if some listeners feel that the 'end' of this first movement is not quite final enough, they may be sure that they are in the right frame of mind. The only real end is the end of the symphony, and the movements should follow each other with very little pause in between.

The *Allegro espansivo* is by far Nielsen's most brilliant and highly wrought achievement to this date; there are, indeed, few (if any) contemporary works that can rival it in the way it blends vivid power with subtlety and depth of feeling, while its tonal organization is of an order of the greatest rarity. As the close reader will have discovered, there is only one way to analyse music of this calibre (or, indeed, any music for that matter): that is from point to point, as a living process in time. One can imagine what a nightmarish problem Nielsen would have posed to a theorist like Schenker, with his static conception of musical form.

The end of the first movement was in A major, but with an effort; A minor was really stronger. The slow movement, *Andante pastorale*, resumes the process by starting in C major, which is closely related to A minor and which, it will be remembered, played an important part in the first movement. In form this piece is utterly individual and, like its precursor, has no independent structure of its own, though it is based on a rising series of pedal points. This series ends with one of the subtlest strokes of genius in Nielsen's works. English listeners will find some affinity between the mood of this music and parts of Vaughan Williams's *Pastoral Symphony* or *The Lark Ascending*; the chief (and fundamental) difference, apart from native stylistic ones, is that whereas Vaughan Williams's works in this vein are totally static, Nielsen passes through the mood as a stage in an active process.

After an introductory phrase from the horns, there glides a long, wandering string melody, unharmonized except for the pedal drone; the quotation gives only the first third of its ruminative course, and as a whole it is, despite its apparent meandering, excellently shaped:

Ex. 23

At Fig. 2 the pedal rises by a major third to E, over which a new thought occurs, reminiscent in shape (not feeling) of part of the *Andante* of Brahms's first Symphony:

Ex. 24

This fragment floats about among the woodwind and is (eleven bars later) interrupted by a passionate outburst from the strings, taking the following phrase as its starting-point:

Ex. 25

During this intense passage the tonality is in a state of flux; it lasts thirteen bars, and at Fig. 5 the bass emerges on a pedal G, a minor third above the previous E. Over this G, Ex. 24 drifts in again with some more very beautiful woodwind writing. Nielsen seems to have had a special affection for woodwind instruments and a very precise appreciation of their individual 'temperaments.' The atmosphere becomes less tranquil as little chromaticisms creep into the counterpoint, and then the strings, this time high up, break in with even greater intensity, one of the few pieces of high string writing in Nielsen that bring Sibelius to mind; the resemblance, however, is superficial. Six bars before Fig. 7, while this string passage is still in being, the bass insists for three bars on B flat, a minor third above the last pedal point, G. Soon after, at Fig. 7 itself, the pedal is on D, a major third higher than B flat. Again Ex. 24 is woven into flowing, disturbed, woodwind counterpoints and then, *Un poco di più animato*, a powerful pedal F makes a *ff* attack, with a hint of Ex. 23, in close canon between lower strings and lower wind.

To review the movement's course so far: there has been a series of pedals, rising by minor and major thirds; C, E, G, B flat, D, F . . . now what? The next step in the series should be nothing less than A itself. The drum tries to hold to F in readiness for the expected rise, but the melody (with the harmony) begins to slip mysteriously downwards, step by step, until it hovers on B flat, taking the drum with it. Then, at Fig. 8, *the whole orchestra*, playing very softly, begins to glow with subdued lustre in the warm sunset light of *E flat major*. This enchanted region is, of course, the opposite pole from A, and it is here that the slow movement stays. The passage is literally at the centre of the symphony, and the expansive nature of the whole work is typified by its magical supplanting of the expected A major. To give added point and poetry to it by making it doubly memorable, two wordless voices, soprano and baritone, weave gracious *melismata* about each other while the orchestra quietly combines Ex. 23 with Ex. 24. The pure E flat major is enriched and relieved by one short passage of deeply expressive, dark harmony between Figs. 11 and 12, then it returns, with voices, before the light fades with a drowsily-sinuous sound from the flutes. Carl Nielsen was not fond of Debussy, but there may be the slightest touch of his influence in the closing bars.

The slow movement carries the ear to the furthest possible remove from A, from the world of action to the warmth and peace of the soothing, gentle roll of Danish fields in high summer. It is profoundly true of this honest, clear-minded man that he regards these two worlds as compatible, even mutually necessary: not for him is any romantic yearning for virtual annihilation in some fancy world of blissful suspended animation; nor does he seek the other so-called 'realistic' extreme, the harsh workaday modern world that (if one is to believe the pessimistic outpourings of self-pity bestowed on the world by so many 'sensitive' modern artists) contains nothing but noise and viciousness. For Nielsen, both ways of life are real, and he can live and understand them both; rest and activity are healthily related, and he has no need to fly either to mysticism or to self-lacerating 'realism.'

Next comes an *Allegretto un poco*, a steady-paced scherzo whose 'main' key is a grey, indeterminate-sounding C sharp minor: but the very indecisiveness of this key is the clue to the movement's transitional character. C sharp minor is nearer to A than to E flat, but the opening bare fifth on horns, coming after the E flat close of the *Andante*, sounds like D flat and A flat (= C sharp and G sharp), especially in view of Nielsen's fondness for the flat seventh. The horns begin loudly (like Viking lurs?), but die away into the following half-lit theme on an oboe:

Ex. 26

At Fig. 1 livelier figures intervene in B major (note this key) and provoke a *fortissimo* containing two important elements:

This strong gesture suggests that the movement will be by no means trifled with, and it flares out in a series of shakes on the dominant of B. It dies away. Instead of a close in B, however, there is a disconcerting change of key to G major, at Fig. 3, with a new, expansive oboe theme, beginning thus:

Ex. 28

Why this tonal vacillation? Because B major and G major are another pair of 'contradictory' keys, each a major third away from E flat. In case this idea seems fanciful Nielsen confirms it (after a fuller counterstatement of Ex. 28) by turning unmistakably to the dominant of E flat at Fig. 5. The music has, in fact, never really left E flat, but is heaving itself about in preparation to do so: hence the introductory feeling of all of it up to Fig. 5, where it starts really to move. In E flat begins a purposeful *fugato* on Ex. 27(*b*); there are three entries, tonic, dominant, tonic; the E flat cannot make up its mind whether to be major or minor and allows other harmonies to invade it. The tension grows and a *crescendo* reaches the region of F sharp minor. At Fig. 7 muted horns cut in angrily and the music moves testily from one harmony to another, eventually settling, none too happily, in D flat (= C sharp) six bars before Fig. 8.

From Fig. 8 there sets out a new expedition, starting off in the direction of A flat minor (the dominant minor of D flat). Now the old tendency reasserts itself, and by Fig. 10 the far pole from A flat minor, the key of D minor, has been reached. This is brought about by an energetic second *fugato* on Ex. 27(*b*), beginning at Fig. 9 in G major; the successive entries of the subject come with fine effect on different beats and the cumulative result of the constant throb of semiquavers and the increasing thud of off-beat accents is a gathering excitement. At Fig. 10 the dominant of D is attained, and a bar later Ex. 28 is heard trying to form itself in D minor through the rising tumult. Gradually and majestically a really magnificent climax is raised, culminating in the clearest D major at Fig. 12. Here is the apex of the piece, establishing D major beyond any doubt; having accomplished this, the movement slips back into its shell (C sharp minor) with the neutral tones of Ex. 26. What was introductory in the first place now assumes the aspect of a coda, which, with warm passing memories of B major, G major, and the barest touch of E flat, brings the movement to its end in the twilight in which it began. At the very finish there is a *tierce de Picardie* as flutes, in the manner of the last moments of the slow movement, hover chromatically round the third of the chord.

For all its strangeness of design the *Allegretto* is an extremely purposeful, massive affair: its subtleties are all of a type with those in the rest of the symphony, and it occupies a kind of tonal no man's land between E flat and A, its chief object being to drive home a forceful climax in D major before resuming its neutrality. The climax itself is one of the most impressive parts of the symphony, and no one feels any surprise when the finale opens cheerfully in D major.

The overall plan is now becoming clear. As the first movement swung from D (minor) to A, so is this last going to do the same; but D major is much more directly related to A major than is D minor. The simplicity of the main tune is of a kind not cared for greatly by those intelligentsia who, in these times of desperate circumspection, cannot see how a man can express deep feelings without being psychologically in need of attention. Tovey (whose ability to find musical subtleties can scarcely be questioned) remarked that there are some people who see so instantly through a thing that they have no time to see into it. But it is usually the subtletyhunters themselves who become infuriated when a composer who, if he liked, could beat them at their own game, has the courage to write a thumping honest tune like this, that makes Holst's *Jupiter* seem cold and mirthless:

Ex. 29

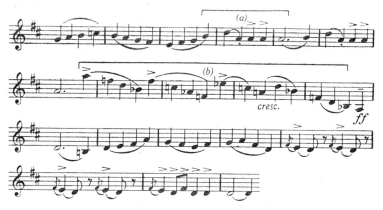

The infuriated ones are, of course, much too scornful to notice that the bass (unquoted) is playing tonic and dominant the 'wrong' way round; if, however, they are still willing to listen, they are strongly advised to take sharp notice of the four bars marked (b) and to wait for their return at the end of the symphony. The sequel to this theme is a swinging subject (obviously suitable for contrapuntal treatment) based on the inversion of Ex. 29(a): the line above it on horns and violas seems at first more important, but it is this bass that Nielsen uses systematically:

Ex. 30

Ex. 30(x) and (y) become active by themselves later on. With easy momentum the music strides along for thirty-four more bars, happily developing Ex. 30; the harmony becomes more colourful, and then at Fig. 4 a new theme, clearly meant to sound like a second subject, begins plaintively in B flat minor. Its chromatic twist is very typical of this composer:

At its ninth bar there is a reference to Ex. 29(*b*) that should be remembered: its influence is slightly disturbing, and the key changes to F sharp minor at Fig. 5, with a counterstatement of Ex. 31. Why this new shift of key? The F sharp minor does not sound very stable, and betrays some anxiety in a rather clamorous climax at Fig. 6: the temperature soon drops, however, and the music falls, apparently relieved, into what seems like a quiet close to the exposition in F sharp major. But why? By now the listener may be prepared for the fact that Nielsen is doing exactly the same thing as he did in the first stages of the *Allegretto*: B flat and F sharp are 'contradictory' in relation to the opening D, just as B and G were 'contradictory' relative to E flat;[1] each of the new keys is a major third away from the original tonic. Thus neither is stable, and in the same way that he returned to E flat in the third movement, so here Nielsen moves back towards D major (page 124 in the score). It looks as if this finale is to be a simple rondo.

Instead of another appearance of the main tune, however, the D major turns into B minor; there is a silent pause, then Ex. 29(*a*) trots in in E minor on an oboe, with a strutting accom-paniment on two bassoons. The piccolo joins, with a

---

[1] And (in the first movement) C sharp and F relative to A.

characteristic extension of the figure into repeated notes, like some articulate hen. An active bass (page 125) begins to develop along with this figure, as the key becomes G major; at Fig. 7 a form of the main theme starts to shape itself in B major, which soon shows itself to be the dominant of E, the lower parts (violas and clarinets, cellos and basses) becoming more and more lively. Eight bars before Fig. 8 the tonality seems to be shifting in the direction of F, but by the ninth bar *after* Fig. 8 the trend of the whole passage is made clear by a huge augmented statement of the first phrase of Ex. 29 in a bold E major.

So far the finale has pursued a simple but totally unpredictable course. D major was soundly established, not only by the great tune itself, but also by the subsequent contradiction of B flat minor by F sharp minor and the move back towards D after that. Now if Nielsen had treated the movement as a simple sonata rondo and brought in the tune again in D at this point, the whole thing would have gone to sleep at once, as well as losing all hope of ever establishing A major. For D major is the subdominant of A. That the movement is wide awake is proved by the immediate turn to E minor (and its dominant) in the development (including a move towards F, the opposite pole of B, which is the dominant of E), followed by this powerful assertion of E major that comes as a climax. The point of the entire passage is that E major is the dominant of A, and it is now fixed with such firmness that no disturbance can do more than shift it from its position as a tonic in its own right and make it behave as a dominant. This is exactly what Nielsen now sets out to do.

The E major climax dies away in a haze of glory that is very reminiscent of Dvořák; notice the oboe part on page 135 and see how its repeated notes turn subtly into a hint of the second subject. At Fig. 9 the ubiquitous repeated notes try to form a *fugato*, and the effect is like that of birds that, having been disturbed by some surprise, wheel gracefully round, and settle

again.   But (although they have no idea of this) they settle on a
different tree, for the earth has apparently turned through half a
rotation under them, and they are in the opposite hemisphere
(B flat).   But something is not quite as it was; that is obvious,
and the second theme (Ex. 31) stirs itself uneasily without
leaving the key of B flat minor.   The whole passage is completely static, expectant; scarcely a leaf moves.   An oboe and
bassoon remember the first phrase of the first subject, but in B
flat, and it fades out.   But from time to time an A flat has crept
in (think of it as G sharp and the idea will begin to dawn).
B flat is only the flat supertonic of A, after all.   As if in proof
that not even birds can defy gravity, action starts all at once in
what is now the home subdominant, D major, with a *fugato* on
Ex. 30, and all the old smiling ease of movement returns,
growing in energy.   Nothing can now prevent the building
of a climax, with many passing inflexions of harmony (not
really of key) during which Ex. 30(x) and (y) act as free agents.
The culmination is, of course, the great main theme, now in
possession of the whole world in a vivid A major that is here
fully established for the first time in the symphony.   But is it
exactly the same tune?   Look at it again: the second subject
took over the passage marked (*b*) in Ex. 29; very well then, the
big tune will return the compliment, and those four bars are
removed to make room for the first phrase of the second subject
(Ex. 31; see four bars before Fig. 12), which flows in so
spontaneously that it is hardly noticed in the general enthusiasm.
But it makes all the difference to the swing of the melody, and
is a perfect demonstration of the way Nielsen's 'repetitions'
are, in fact, actively constructive memories.

  Works by other composers that appeared about 1910–11:
Ravel, *Daphnis et Chloé*; Busoni, *Die Brautwahl*, Sonatina
No. 1, *Fantasia contrappuntistica*; Vaughan Williams, *A Sea
Symphony*, Fantasia on a Theme of Thomas Tallis, and *Hugh
the Drover* (begun); Debussy begins *Préludes* for piano; Strauss,

Aged forty-three

Der Rosenkavalier; Stravinsky, *L'Oiseau de feu* and *Petrouchka*; Delius, *Summer Night on the River* and *On Hearing the First Cuckoo in Spring* (1911–12); Schoenberg, *Pierrot lunaire*, *Erwartung*, *Die Glückliche Hand*, and completion of *Gurrelieder* (all between 1909 and 1912); Bloch, *Macbeth*; Scriabin, *Prometheus*; Elgar, violin Concerto and second Symphony; Mahler, *Das Lied von der Erde*; Sibelius, Symphony No. 4; Saint-Saëns, *Déjanire*.

F

CHAPTER V

THE FOURTH SYMPHONY

(*The Inextinguishable*)

1914–16

BETWEEN the violin Concerto (which belongs to the period of the *Sinfonia espansiva*) and his next symphony, No. 4, Nielsen wrote the sinewy 'G minor' violin Sonata (the second), Op. 35; it shows a marked toughening in his spirit, with a definite element of conflict coming to the fore. This sonata was written in 1912. As if to balance his growing sense of foreboding, he occupied himself throughout 1913 with less important matters, but the next year and, no doubt, the outbreak of war on a large scale, brought out all that had been accumulating within. In 1914 he began *The Inextinguishable*: Symphony No. 4. Also, by way of contrast, he commenced his memorable collaboration with Thomas Laub on the delightful collection of settings of native Danish poetry. The fourth Symphony absorbed him until the beginning of 1916, during which time he was able to work at very little else; once the symphony was finished, however, he wrote quite quickly two of his best piano works, the *Chaconne* and the *Theme and Variations*, both of which share in different degrees the symphony's steely power.

The conflict depicted in this work is the inevitable upshot of the composer's broadening, maturing outlook. The third Symphony displays the cross-currents that inform any genuinely organic growth, but it is entirely filled with the sheer joy of living.   In No. 4 Nielsen gives vent to his feelings about life in general: as a man of the soil, he was naturally deeply moved by the vast spectacle of life in all its forms, its incessant fight for existence, and, above all, its unmistakably purposive evolution: he was impressed, too, by its extraordinary capacity for surviving, in some form, almost any catastrophe.   The name of the fourth Symphony therefore refers, not to the composer's opinion of his own composition, but to a clear-cut feeling that he found he could express with peculiar accuracy in music.

Again he finds the fundamental facts of tonality profoundly capable of expressing his idea, and the symphony evolves the key of E major out of apparent chaos: every stage in the process is faithfully and spontaneously reflected in the details of the music.   At no time is there any trace of pedantry or slavishness to a 'programme'; such faults always arise from a naïvety that Nielsen has left far behind.   As the third Symphony was held together by an overall tonal structure, so this work takes the next step by being actually continuous.   There are four distinct movements, but they are interlinked, and none is in any sense self-sufficient.

The music at once hurls the hearer into the heart of a flaming nebula, from which order is to grow: with explosive violence it plunges *in medias res* with two conflicting streams of fire, one (woodwind) centred round D and the other (strings) round C. The quotation gives the bare essentials:

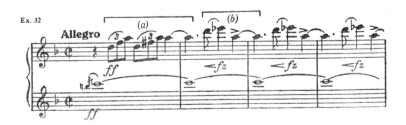

The drums enforce the sound of the tritone, E flat⁀A. As will be heard, the last part of the quotation shows that C has momentarily got the upper hand, but this is a mere instant in the turmoil. The figures (*b*), (*c*), and (*d*) together boil up a fierce climax, rushing into this formation four bars after Fig. 2:

Ex. 33

The time suddenly broadens out into 5–2, then 3–2: the
actual high point is at Fig. 3, after which darkness swallows
the flames, and the whole expires defiantly on the dominant of
A (consecutive 'unrelated' triads descending impressively over
a pedal E).   The real tonal focus of this strife has been D
minor, not C: but C, being Nielsen's favourite flat seventh in
D minor, is associated with it again in due course.   For the
fourth time he has begun a symphony with a powerful opening
tutti; this is the last time, for the remaining two symphonies
begin softly.   This *tutti* is also somewhat shorter even than
that of No. 2, being a rather quicker thirty-two bars: the
strength and depth here are, of course, far greater.

As the music fades out, Ex. 33 flickers dimly in the woodwind, with Ex. 32(*b*) answering below on a solo cello.   Then
in A major, the clarinets play a long, arching theme that
suggests calmness and order:

Ex. 34

The strings take it up, and it immediately begins to form its own ramifications by finding new phrases (see the continuation from Fig. 6). After Fig. 7 it begins to hesitate, touching the alien dominant of A flat minor: violas, then violins, curl mysteriously upwards; violas accent the note E flat with repeated notes in a *diminuendo* (an effect that should be remem⹀ bered); clarinets try to start Ex. 34 again in A flat minor. But the effect of A major is still strong enough to brush this aside: there is an abrupt outburst of an exultant march⹀like derivative of Ex. 34 in E major. This is the first appearance of this key, towards which the whole symphony is driving; at present it is felt merely as the dominant of A, and its in⹀ security is made plain by the turn to A flat in its fifth bar. This *risoluto e giusto* passage becomes more strenuous as with an *accelerando* it tumbles precipitately into C major, where the brass (*Tempo I*) attempt to raise a new climax on Ex. 34: with the entry of the woodwind, the harmony brightens and the exposition, turning into A major in the nick of time, carries home triumphantly in that key the substance of Ex. 34, treated antiphonally in a passage marked, typically, *pesante ma glorioso*. At Fig. 11 the theme stalks majestically down through two octaves; notice Nielsen's complete unself⹀consciousness in giving 'grace⹀notes' to the trombones. The end of the exposition is a *diminuendo*.

All is quiet, except for the faint rhythm of a drum below the sustained A major chords; the rhythm is that of Ex. 32(*b*), and a flute very softly uses it to sow discord. A horn answers, with the deliberate object of pulling the tonality back to D minor; the rhythmic fragments gather themselves grimly together and the drum is dislodged from A to D *(poco più vivo*, page 19). The atmosphere becomes ominous. Violins pick up the rhythm and keep it going with all kinds of harsh intervals, still *pianissimo*. Below them, at intervals, violas mutter tensely the repeated notes last heard just before the march⹀like passage in E major. At first (Fig. 13) they strike D, and though they start *ff*, they peter out both rhythmically and dynamically. At their third attack, basses answer with an augmentation of Ex. 32(*a*) and (*b*), but in E, *ppp*. Meanwhile the violins keep up their dissonant, but still soft, interference, gradually removing their mutes. Again comes the persistent D on the violas; this time the basses make the same reply, but a semi-tone higher. Taking this hint, the violas assert an E flat and basses answer still another semitone higher, in F sharp. Then violas go up one more to E; at the sound of this note, the violins, challenged, leap into a ferocious *fortissimo*. The wind instruments enter with harsh trills (a passage that is foreshadowed in the corresponding place in the first movement of the violin Sonata, Op. 35), and then the whole orchestra plunges into a veritable convulsion of fury, in which the key of E strives to survive against a mass of conflicting counter-points. Ex. 32(*a*) is heard in two keys in the lower registers, G and E (both minor and major), while high above a hurricane seems to howl in a strange canon-like effect; through all the tremendous uproar, the piccolo pierces like lightning with Ex. 32(*b*).[1] At Fig. 18 the dominant of E is heard, and whether by design or coincidence it matters not, the bass actually turns Ex. 32(*a*) into something remarkably like the theme of the *Allegro sanguineo* of the second Symphony. It cannot easily be heard, but it is odd that this reference, if such it be, should occur at the point when the dominant of E is first sounded.

Gradually this storm spends itself in a series of waves, broken up by dramatically bare interruptions from Ex. 34, which has lost sight of E major, and is tossed to and fro by powerful surging treatments of the triplet figure by the full orchestra. At length the restful key of G major is reached (the far side, as

---

[1] I can never hear this fearsome passage without visualizing that mild and friendly man, Johan Bentzon, his microscopic piccolo shining bright in front of his great dark beard.

it were, of D and a relative of E minor), and in this key Ex. 34 tries to form itself, lapped gently by the triplet rhythm, now very soothing in the strings. At Fig. 22 comes a deep sigh and a modulation sinking into C; again, in a section of great and luminous beauty, Ex. 34 tries to grow and flower. But in this context, C major is an extremely dangerous key: it is as if the evolutionary process had fallen into an almost fatally pleasant backwater. As a result the air is disturbed again by a struggling *crescendo*, and the recapitulation crashes in, this time in an unequivocal D minor. A severe effort must be made, or the first movement may not be able to move away from its starting point.

The key of E makes an attempt to take control at the fifth bar after Fig. 24, but it is not secure enough, and acts as dominant to A (fourth bar, page 38). At Fig. 25, with a thunder of drums and trombones, the key rises a major third to C sharp (written as D flat); seven bars later this almost closes into E major but is (in a very literal sense) flatly contra-dicted by Ex. 32(*d*) in E flat minor. This turns to its relative major, G flat, which calls itself F sharp; F sharp is the domi-nant of B, which is the dominant of E: there is a great blaze of excitement, and at Fig. 27 E major successfully drives home the striding version of Ex. 34 that ended the exposition. Thus the whole of this restatement is fused into a single incandescent *fortissimo*, full of strife, yet brightening continuously towards a partial establishment of E major. There is a *diminuendo* as the recapitulation gives rise to expectations of a coda. But E major, though it has not been definitely fixed, has cleared the air sufficiently to allow some relaxation, and instead of a coda to complete the first movement, there comes a delicately scored interlude in G major, led into by a long, hesitating violin line over a soft drum (notice that the drum, in recognition of the true nature of the E major that has just been heard, falls after a few bars to A).

The woodwind are given great freedom and the movement can be compared formally (though not stylistically) with the gentle *allegretto* pieces that Brahms substitutes for the normal scherzo. This key of G has been previously hinted at in the first movement; the structure of this piece is simply AA_2BA, but its periods are exquisitely proportioned, with finely balanced irregularities that are as unpredictable as the behaviour of children or the shapes of flowers. The evolution of life is not a wholly turbulent process, and its quieter side is reflected here. As in the first movement, the G major is really the dominant of C, in which the section 'B' is cast; between the two keys is 'A_2,' in a Neapolitan D flat major. Here is the delightful winding first sentence:

Ex. 35

The woodwind writing in this *intermezzo* is characteristic, anticipating in some ways the lovely wind Quintet of 1922: the changes of time are unobtrusive but effective. Ten bars before Fig. 28 is a passage that seems to articulate the very sounds of birds and insects on a warm summer day (another, twelve bars before Fig. 29, is even more evocative). At Fig. 28 a new version of Ex. 35 is heard on oboes and clarinets in D

flat (this is the start of 'A₂'); this D flat is only the flat supertonic of C, in which the 'middle' section is set, beginning at
Fig. 29 with a soft new idea on *pizzicato* strings.   Over this
comes a floating phrase on an oboe, as soft as possible, and it
expands into delicate fronds.   The rhythm eventually hints at
the beginning of Ex. 35, and the first part returns with a slight
change of harmony that brings the end back into G major
(the section originally ended in B flat, so that that key and D
flat fall into place as flat seventh and flat supertonic in respective
relation to C major).

As the last clarinet notes fall away the violins break sharply
in with an intense *cantilena*, forming a long, taut line accompanied only by heavy, dry *pizzicati* and drum strokes.   The key
is struggling to be E major:

Ex. 36   **Poco adagio quasi andante**

Violas and cellos take it up in the dominant and the bareness
of the counterpoint is accentuated by the gradual cessation of
the severe accompaniment.   Were it not for the enormous

scale of the subject one might think this is to be a slow fugue, but it soon becomes clear that Nielsen has neither time nor inclination for this, as he is much more intent on following the inevitable tonal conflict to its end; a slow fugue, immediately after the calm *allegretto*, would, however tense its mood, kill the dramatic life of the work at this point.   At length relief comes, and a solo violin (helped by Ex. 36(*b*), now turned into a bird-like cry) plays in the frankest E major the following beautiful phrase without the slightest hint of sentimentality:

Ex. 37

p espress.

The full strings dwell on this: then the key of E begins to lose its hold; developing the same serene phrase, the music drifts through foreign keys in the direction of C major, where it appears to be settling (Fig. 35 et seq.).   As in the first movement, C major is a dangerously blissful region, and the woodwind interject a loud warning with Ex. 36(*c*), off-key (dominant of B): impressively answered by solemn trombone harmonies (on Ex. 37), the warning is repeated half a tone higher, solo string instruments waiting anxiously with Ex. 36(*b*). By now there is enough tension in the air to allow a fugue to develop without holding up the action, and Ex. 36(*c*) forms itself into a close-knit, determined *fugato*; there is an elemental Old Testament dignity in its severity.   As the tension grows, Ex. 37 appears suddenly on the horns in the key of F a bar before Fig. 38, and in augmented form on the trombones in the very next bar.   The strings coalesce into powerful octaves and a great climax is slowly reared, with Ex. 36(*b*) penetrating the waves of counterpoint with its persistent bird-cry.   At Fig. 39 the texture hardens and the harmony becomes even more urgent: the actual climax comes five bars later, a blaze of brass and drums in E major. That key is now, as such, fully established, but the vital thematic factor, Ex. 34, is missing (it may not be superfluous to mention at this point that although tonality is of the greatest importance in Nielsen's work, he does not believe in the significance of a key that has no connection with musical invention). Without this theme, E major can be said to be only tentatively asserted. So the sound fades again into a deep reflective calm, not without suspense (Fig. 40), where elements of Ex. 36(*a*) and (*b*) and Ex. 37 float uncertainly about, passing through A minor and A flat minor. Then Ex. 36(*c*), on an oboe, hangs magically among glim‑mering trills in the strings.

All at once there is a *crescendo*, and the violins flash into vivid, mercurial life (Fig. 42); the other strings join, finding the dominant of A minor, horns reinforce the note E and the drums drive it home. There is a silent bar and the finale springs out in A major. This passage is obviously a descendant of the famous example in Beethoven's *Leonora* No. 3. The spirit, too, is similar, and it is a mark of Nielsen's greatness that he is bold enough to risk the comparison. In this he is bolder even than Vaughan Williams who, in his fourth Symphony (the vitriolic F minor), links scherzo and finale in the manner of Beethoven's fifth: in the case of the English composer the temper of his music is so utterly removed from that of the original example that the comparison is almost irrelevant. Here, however, the heroic character of the music is distinctly akin to Beethoven's, and the risk of comparison is therefore much greater. But both Nielsen and Vaughan Williams are of sufficient stature to take such risks.

The last movement opens with a long, expansive melody containing references to Ex. 34, Ex. 36(*b*), and Ex. 37, all absorbed into its cogent line with the completest spontaneity:

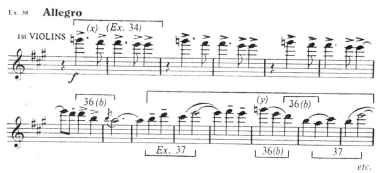

Its majestic confidence is soon shattered by disruptive rhythms and dissonances (Fig. 44), out of which emerges this angry theme:

The tonality becomes obscured by its harshness and the mood gets increasingly destructive with strange dislocations and violences in all parts of the orchestra: at Fig. 47 the scene is ready for the entry of a new and formidable character—a second pair of timpani. In a footnote the composer instructs both timpanists to maintain a menacing tone, even in *piano* passages: this foreshadows his astonishing use of the side-drum in the fifth Symphony, described in the next chapter. There is a deep reason for Nielsen's delaying of this threatening element until so late in the symphony; it is only at a certain stage in an evolutionary process that sharply opposed dominating forces crystallize themselves. The social evolution of man is at present reaching such a crisis, and conflict on this level (to be found throughout the fifth Symphony) is far more terrible than the diffused competitive strife of the jungle. The widening objectivity of Carl Nielsen's view has now reached the point when he is able to analyse the human struggle in which he himself (by virtue of his very existence) is a partisan, and to depict it in accurate and unmistakable terms. Thus such music as this is not 'programme music' in the nine-teenth-century sense, but is the organic product of an age; its 'programme' is its faithfulness to experience, not to windy philosophy.

The drums crash in at Fig. 47, each pair hammering a tritone, and the four making a diminished seventh: a turbulent struggle ensues, filled with deeds both dark and glorious (the listener will define these for himself). At Fig. 48 triplet rhythms that hint at the opening of the first movement dominate a heaving passage in F sharp minor; at Fig. 49 comes a mighty clash of swords based on Ex. 38(x), with terrific slashing chords on the strings. The drums enter the arena again and the orchestra breaks in, with the tension at its highest, in B flat; the music tugs itself out of this key and succeeds in bursting over into A major at last, fully in command of one of Nielsen's magnificent *glorioso* passages (Fig. 50). This dies away into a long stretch of soft preparation, filled with the characteristic tense repeated notes that occur in almost all his works. The keys pass fitfully like clouds across a plain, and one has the sense that the end is in sight; A major is at least half way from D minor to E major. At Fig. 54 there is a real gleam of distant light as the key of B major is reached (the dominant of E); here there is a wonderful hushed canonic treatment of Ex. 38(y), like a soft fresh wind blowing. Inevitably, suggestions of Ex. 34 begin to float across the scene (six bars after Fig. 57); their connections with Ex. 38(x) also become apparent. All this material, with two newer fragments that grew during the previous passage of preparation (one rising and falling, the other derived from it, but with an expressive chromatic dip), goes to make one of Nielsen's most beautiful stretches of music, full of extraordinary grace and subdued power.

But the conflict is not over, and in anticipation of the final crisis, the mood becomes deeper and more solemn. With a slight hastening (*Più mosso*, page 97), the B major is reduced to minor; then the drums deliver a last attack (Fig. 59). Here is another deep subtlety, if such a word can be used to describe anything so violent; between them the four drums form a chord of D minor, the key openly associated with chaos at the start of the work. The conflict is now at its starkest, simplest opposition. Against the D minor din of the drums, the violins and woodwind repeatedly fling out the note B, the dominant of E. To their aid come horns and trumpets with the spur of Ex. 34, and the harmony is rent with dissonance. At this point of highest stress (two bars before Fig. 61) the drums are precipitately wrenched from their D minor (notice their *glissandi*); then the choleric Ex. 39 tears itself free and sweeps irresistibly into a complete and final statement of Ex. 34 in an unassailable E major.

As will have been noticed, this symphony is easier to analyse than its emotionally simpler predecessor; the reason is that the issues involved are more sharply defined. The result is an illustration of the fact that in Nielsen's work there is a steady progress in the integration of form and content. The philosophical or emotional origins of this fourth Symphony are deeper, more complex than those that produced No. 3, but they are more consciously understood by the composer, who is therefore able to reflect them more accurately in the construction of the music. *The Inextinguishable* is one of Nielsen's most concentrated works; its position in his output may be compared roughly with that of the *Eroica* or the C minor in Beethoven's (without, of course, attempting any closer parallel): there are in Nielsen's own works perhaps only three that surpass it, the fifth Symphony, the colossal first movement of the sixth, and the great organ composition, *Commotio*. The broadest and most salient of its themes (Ex. 34) has been unfavourably compared with the famous swinging minim subject in the finale of Sibelius's E flat Symphony, No. 5, but such a criticism is extremely superficial; it takes no account of the fact that the two ideas have nothing whatever in common. Sibelius's is a simple *ostinato*, of more rhythmic than melodic significance; on no account can it be called a distinguished piece of musical invention in itself, and it is one of those admirably platitudinous tags on which a great master can erect a superb structure. Nielsen's theme, on the other hand, is a fully developed melody, and Ex. 34 is not the whole of it; it is not meant to behave at any time as an *ostinato*, and it is heard complete only twice during the whole symphony. Even this is not quite true, for it would be fair to say that the fully formed melody is not heard at all until the very end; at its first appearance its close is enormously delayed by all that occurs between Fig. 6 and Fig. 11, so that it is scarcely felt as a whole. Only in the final section, in E major, is it securely bound together as an entity. Thus one cannot find a point of contact between the two things; those who find the dogged repetitions of the Sibelius tedious may feel a more spontaneously musical impulse behind Nielsen's idea, and those who prefer the Finn's special brand of economy may find the Dane too uninhibited. But there is much to be said for understanding them both without trying to play off one against the other.

In 1923, Carl Nielsen came to London and conducted a concert of his own music in Queen's Hall, with the London Symphony Orchestra; the programme included the fourth Symphony. Torben Meyer gives two amusing anecdotes about this visit in his biographical appendix on pages 204–5, but it may be of interest to quote here two press criticisms of the symphony. First, Edwin Evans in the *Pall Mall Gazette*, June 1923:

. . . the most serious number was the symphony (*The Inextinguishable*), a strongly personal utterance, the very sincerity of which precluded all concessions to superficial effect.   In consequence, it is austere, even bleak, music, such as will not appeal to the sensuous.   It is in four continuous movements in the usual sequence, and the slow section is very impressive. This is constructed of broad epic phrases, presented naked of harmonic colouring and punctuated by two timpanists [sic!], one of whom is placed at the side of the orchestra.   The mood thus expressed is maintained with increased vigour in the finale.   It is of northern character throughout.

His anonymous colleague on *The Times* is less perceptive and uses conventional stock phrases:

Mr. Nielsen's music has behind it the solidity of classical tradition, together with the evidences of an enterprising invention.   The symphony No. 4, called *The Inextinguishable*, in four linked movements, has some striking moments.   The irregular woodwind-rhythm of the *Poco allegretto* was quite captivating, and the strong outline of the *Adagio* following it was quite arresting.   There is a cold, northern feeling about the orchestration, particularly in the bare use of single instruments.

These two quotations are evidence that the reception of Nielsen in London at that time was cordial enough to make one think that if he had been able to return and give two or three more concerts, nearly thirty years of neglect in England might have been prevented.   It is interesting to see that the critics were first struck by the 'cold,' 'northern' quality of the music, and it would have been easier for them, perhaps, if he had chosen to introduce the *Sinfonia espansiva* to them.   After a lapse of twenty-eight years, in 1951, the fourth Symphony was again played in London, this time by the Danish State Radio Symphony Orchestra under Launy Grøndahl.   It is illuminating to compare the reaction of *The Times* with the above extract from 1923: one must, of course, take into account the fact that the 1951 performance was probably greatly superior to the earlier one, even though that had the benefit of the composer's direction; the London Symphony Orchestra can scarcely have had time to get accustomed to the unfamiliar

G

idiom, while the Danish orchestra was playing its own music almost, it seemed, from memory. But there can be no doubt of the impact the symphony made at this Festival Hall performance:

> Certainly the quality of the symphony's thought is energy; the opening of the work is hurled at us with tremendous energy, the climax of the development is suffused in it, and it bursts through the finale. The whole frame of the symphony quivers with the vigour which propels it from the beginning to the end of a vast and impassioned musical sentence. As in the fifth Symphony, which this orchestra played at Edinburgh last year, orchestral colour is applied liberally, but with striking individuality. The finale is dominated by two sets of timpani, separately disposed, which crash out their challenges alternately; between the two outer move-ments, woodwind takes charge in a graceful movement of the Brahms scherzo-substitute kind, and strings in a tense and fiery slow movement. Passages there are that do not captivate the hearer of themselves, but these are carried along in the flow of Nielsen's enthusiasm—and the enthusiasm of his splendid interpreters.

How ardently *The Times* desires to be captivated! A similar tone was maintained at this time by almost all the other critics,[1] and this concert consolidated what had been achieved in Edinburgh with the fifth Symphony the previous year. The one tragic aspect of it is that the composer could not have lived to witness his music's triumph in the country which, next to his own, he loved most. But although he would have been grateful for the recognition in the press, he would have been far more moved by the tremendous response of the audience that September evening; rarely can an unfamiliar symphony have struck home so directly to an English audience. It is noteworthy that no one had much to say about northern cold-ness, although someone had to make the crackjaw pun about 'The Indigestible.'

In 1915–16 these works, among others, were written:

[1] One of the less inhibited newspapers actually headed its column 'A Knock-out Symphony'!

Schoenberg, *Die Jakobsleiter* (unfinished); Busoni, *Rondo Arlecchinesco*; Bloch, *Schelomo*; Richard Strauss, *Alpine Symphony*; Sibelius, fifth Symphony; Prokofiev, *Chout*; Falla, *Love the Magician* and *Nights in the Gardens of Spain*; Stravinsky, *Les Noces*; Milhaud, *Poème* for piano and orchestra; Reger, Variations and Fugue on a theme of Mozart; Frank Bridge, *Summer*; Bax, *The Garden of Fand*; Holst, *The Planets*; Stanford, piano Concerto No. 2; Vaughan Williams, *A London Symphony* (first version); Miaskovsky, Symphony No. 3; Magnard, Symphony No. 4; Elgar, *Carillon* and *Polonia*.

CHAPTER VI

THE FIFTH SYMPHONY

1920-2

SYMPHONY No. 5, Op. 50, which has no name, was begun in 1920. By this time the war was well over, but its long and painful tragedy had left its mark on Carl Nielsen's mind, even though he lived in a country not drastically affected by it. During the years between 1916 and 1920 he had composed steadily; the chief orchestral music that had come was for the theatre (for *Aladdin* and for *Moderen*), and there was also the exquisite *Pan and Syrinx*, Op. 49, dated 1918. The piano received his best gift to it in 1919, the powerfully original Suite Op. 45. In 1921, as a relief from the arduous task of composing the symphony, he wrote the cantata, *Springtime on Fyn*, one of his most felicitous works. The fifth Symphony proved to be what he himself said was one of the hardest things he had ever tried to do; no wonder, for its originality and its weight of substance are startling, and it penetrates regions that no other composer had explored. He remarked in 1922, after he had finished it, that while most composers were successful enough in managing the first three movements of a normal symphony, many of them 'slipped up' (his own characteristic words) in the finale; he said that he himself often felt that this was a very real problem and wondered if even Beethoven had brought voices into the ninth Symphony because he was afraid he might not succeed with an instrumental finale. But this, like all remarks to the press, was a half-truth; it would have taken him much longer to explain the deeper reasons why this symphony has only two movements.

84

The simple explanation given above would be more convincing if the symphony actually avoided the well-known
problem of the finale. But it does not: it has the greatest finale
in all Nielsen's works. One can, for instance, understand
Mahler's constant fear of the problem, for to him the finale had
to be an apotheosis, and his inability to achieve what was
essentially an unreal idea led to his ninth Symphony ending in
a slow movement. On a lower plane, Tchaikovsky had
similar difficulties. Nielsen's conception of the finale never had
anything in common with that of the romantics: in his first
three symphonies, in the string quartets and in both the violin
sonatas, the finale is never more than life-size, and has a function
much more akin to that of Haydn's or (in some cases) Dvořák's
last movements (there is a strong affinity between the earlier
Nielsen and Dvořák when the latter is not trying to please the
critics). In the fourth and fifth Symphonies, the final movements are heroic, but in no romantic sense: in this he follows
the line of Beethoven, who grew in stature himself before his
music became heroic, so that the music remained life-size,
whatever the force of its content. As soon as writing works
on an heroic scale became a convention, the artistic climate
became fit only for adolescents, so that few composers succeeded
in rising above this level. Nielsen had the sense to realize that
before he could compose works of the widest scope he must
grow up to them.

By the time he came to consider the fifth Symphony he was
fifty-five and his philosophy of life had reached a definitive
stage. The fourth, as has been shown, reflects the evolutionary process; in that work he was concerned with the whole
panorama of biological life, and the music expresses what he
felt about the invincibility of its power to survive. Towards
the end of No. 4 there is something more at stake than mere
survival; the entry of the new pair of drums marks a more
meaningful, *conscious* conflict, a point when the evolving,

entangled processes produce a direct opposition of two dominant forces. This is the point at which the fifth begins; here is

Autograph of the opening of the Fifth Symphony

man's conflict, in which his progressive, constructive instincts
are at war with other elements (also human) that face him with
indifference or downright hostility.

Nielsen found he could best reflect this drama in a two-movement work, the first movement to contain the crux of the conflict itself and the second to be a finale that would rise out of the ashes in a great fount of regenerative energy. Even this finale is not to be free of difficulties, but it is to prove irresistible in the end. The tonal structure of the symphony is apt to every detail of this plan, yet the whole work sounds as if it sprang complete to the composer's mind. Again he uses 'progressive' tonality, and an analysis can do little more than follow the music from point to point. In some ways the work is clearer and easier to follow than almost any previous one by Nielsen; yet its deepest subtleties may well prove limitless. The course of the struggle is plain, for it is the same in which every one is embroiled; a man may disagree with Nielsen's feelings about it, but he will recognize the subject.

The first movement's ground-plan is extremely simple; it partly adopts the technique of the slow movement of the *Sinfonia espansiva*, but with vastly different results. It is constructed upon three immense planes of tonality, rising by fifths, F, C, and G. The opening is quite unlike anything else in this composer's music and, indeed, cannot really be paralleled in any other's. The quiet mysterious opening has been the favourite gambit of every romantic who has misunderstood Beethoven's ninth Symphony; a few masters, like Schubert and Bruckner, have used it in their own ways (still more misunderstood). One is only too sorely familiar with the composer who starts his big work with a weird hum, throb, or drone while he (and the unfortunate audience) waits in vain for something to occur. Never in his life was Nielsen driven to this device until he wanted to convey precisely what many of his precursors unwittingly conveyed—a complete absence of momentum. The beginning is like the passing of time, a background for events. Under a persistent wavy line on violas, bassoons creep in with cold harmonies:

Ex. 40

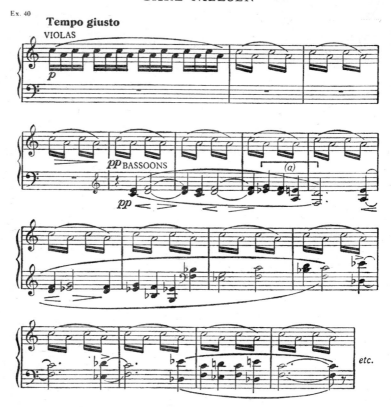

The tonality seems to hover at first round D, F, and C; nothing is determined: the bassoons break into a harsh, meaningless sound, violas hesitate, and then at Fig. 2[1] the horns softly echo Ex. 40(*a*) in D, only to be contradicted by the flutes in C. The two keys eddy round each other and the continuous viola line threads between them, for all the world like the wave of a seismograph that reacts to the tremors of earthquakes at vast distances, then settles to its neutral uniformity:

[1] The numbers refer to the new score published by *Skandinavisk Musikforlag.*

Ex. 41

At Fig. 4, the first violins, muted, slip in almost impercep‐
tibly with a long undulating melody, second violins add them‐
selves to the violas in consecutive fifths, and the bass at last
makes it clear that the key is F.   Here is the beginning of the
first violin line, which moves almost entirely by step in a long,
quietly arching, perfectly still span.

Ex. 42

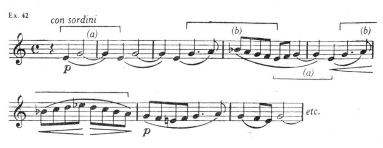

Ex. 41 now 'registers' a stronger warning, with flutes and
clarinets added in bare fourths.   The melody begins again at
the upper octave, this time with disturbing faint accents in the
bass; now it is not able to flow so calmly, and at Fig. 7 it freezes
into hushed, stabbing, repeated notes, echoing below.   A
solitary clarinet picks up the *ostinato* (now on G and F); a cold
shiver runs through the woodwind, and the strings fade away
with a numbed reference to Ex. 42(*a*), as if the emotionless
background were receding before a new influence.   Then
comes the distant sound of a side‐drum beating a simple and
all too plain rhythm: woodwind cry out with Ex. 42(*a*), which
loses its individuality as the timpani and lower strings (*pizzi‐
cato*) turn it into a heavy *ostinato* on the notes D and F, like the
tick of a monstrous clock.   The violins respond with a

tortuous line that still tries to preserve the rise and fall of
Ex. 42(*b*):

Ex. 43

The side-drum relentlessly keeps up its monotonous rhythm
(readers for whom this description stirs long-smothered
memories of the first movement of the *Leningrad* Symphony [1]
need have no fears); the mood becomes wilder and more
desperate as a clarinet and then a flute personify all that is savage
and destructively egotistical.   At Fig. 14 the strings still try to
sustain a line through the dismal din; five bars after, the
clarinet introduces a flying fragment that is to form a new
ostinato:

Ex. 44   CLARINET

All this time the key of F is disappearing and the constant
sound of F and D produces the effect of a D minor that is
always leaning towards the key of C.   This tendency is confirmed three bars before Fig. 16 when the oboes insist upon a
dominant-sounding G, after the turmoil has for the moment
died down and the strings' melody has failed to complete itself.
Then the cellos drive home their low C, and the second great
tonal plane has been reached (Fig. 16, *Tranquillo*).   Meanwhile
Ex. 44 has become a continuous murmur, and the side-drum

        [1] Shostakovich is a much better artist than this inflated work suggests.

is still. Emphasizing that a crucial stage is at hand, the bassoon phrase of Ex. 40 enters, doubled by horns; *it is at the same pitch as before, but is now in C.* Its continuation is different and it moves about restlessly while the bass holds fast to its C; the music remains ominous, with malevolent flickerings of Ex. 44 on flute and clarinet and an occasional tinge of tambourine tone. But the general tendency is to rise, and five bars before Fig. 19 the bass struggles up a semitone to D flat. At this, reactionary wrath is invoked, and the sidedrum and percussion crash in again. The bass, despite this, forces its way upwards and with a great effort gets as far as G flat at Fig. 19. The violins, roused, make a new, strained bid to form a cogent melody; they still preserve recognizable contours of Ex. 42, but painfully distorted, and are crushed by the opposing weight: the line falters and disintegrates. The bass (notice that the cellos have not, through this *mêlée*, had the support of the doublebasses) tries to hang on to G flat, but it loses it: an oboe (Fig. 21) plaintively plays Ex. 41 at the pitch where its central note is F and its upper and lower extremes are A flat and D respectively (this is an important point, and should be remembered). The celesta repeats the note D in a mechanical rhythm derived from the expiring end of the last passage, and the bass, unable to hold G flat, falls again to C (six bars after Fig. 21).

As was mentioned earlier, the tonality of this movement rises through fifths, from F to C and from C to G: the bass has begun its attempts to reach G, but is foiled at G flat. Now follows a profound passage. The oboe extends Ex. 41, the violas and cellos accentuate their held C with a downwardthrusting triplet (F flat, E flat, D flat, to C; really in A flat), and a clarinet gives vent to a wild wailing. The violins join the celesta in its strange 'fixation' on the note D, which stabs through the gloom like a recurrent fog light; flutes and oboes grope for something firm in these tonal quicksands with what sounds at first like the ghost of Ex. 43. Below, the bass heaves in its obscured A flat and the fog thickens. One bar before Fig. 24, the cellos confirm the hint of A flat with a slow rising *arpeggio* of that key (major): at this, clarinets and bassoons play cold A flat major-minor phrases, sphinx-like, while the intermittent D flashes above, a seemingly meaningless signal in a placeless void; yet it is a light. Then everything fades; a flute [1] faintly essays the triplet accent of the bass and the rhythm of the side-drum is remotely heard: all that is left is the still feebly 'visible' light, the pulsing D, with tiny hints of percussion sounds.

A flat and D are 'contradictory' keys: not only are they at opposite poles; there is an extra danger. The mean between them is the inert, energyless region of F. This pair of keys should be kept in mind, for it reappears with fearsome effect in the second movement. What is to come now? Fortunately the last sound to remain was the pinpoint D, for the A flat vanished into the darkness before it. Suddenly there is a sign of life in these deeps and an oboe breaks the tension with the triplet figure; all at once the D is revealed as a beacon of hope, the dominant of G major. In G comes a new theme, full of aspiration and light, at first in the subdued middle tones of the orchestra but soon soaring slowly and majestically higher. The quotation gives only the start of what is an enormous sentence:

So the third tonal plane, G, has been attained at last, and at first (as if to make certain) the theme proceeds over a pedal:

[1] The new score misprints it as oboe at the top of page 43.

but the other troubled regions were tied to pedals, and this section gives its bass much more freedom, holding it to a pedal occasionally instead of all the time.   For the first time in the symphony the texture expands contrapuntally, and it is a strong temptation to place the passage that follows as one of the greatest in the music of this century; there are few contempor‚ aries who can write so mightily as this.   If one describes it as having the solidity of Bach and the dramatic force of Beethoven, this is not because it represents those two unapproachable titans rolled into one, but because no others offer relevant comparison.   Nor is it to dismiss other composers; but the mention of Bach and Beethoven may serve to indicate the quality of this music.

The contrapuntal development of Ex. 45 is carried out in huge waves.   The first of these culminates at Fig. 29, where the tonality brightens into a glorious B major.   There is no point in an academic examination here of the details of Nielsen's counterpoint; it would bear the same kind of close analysis as Tovey gives *The Art of Fugue*, and any one who has a score can see for himself the weaving of Ex. 45 with free parts and in *stretto* with itself.   What is more important is to make clear the high points of tonal tension that mark the progress of the drama.   For the drama is by no means finished.   The blaze of sunlight at the climax of Fig. 29 slowly wanes and by Fig. 31 the key is G major again.   A point to note is that the B major is the opposite pole from F, in which the symphony began.

At Fig. 31 the process flows serenely on again, but this time it is impinged upon by Ex. 41, high in the woodwind.   As before, this has a minatory effect.   Instead of brightening, the music darkens towards the fatal F, actually going into the minor of that key at Fig. 32.   Ex. 41 continually reiterates its warning.   F minor is shaken off and the dominant of G regained at Fig. 33, where the brass make a powerful *stretto* on Ex. 45(a), but in G minor.   Ex. 41 redoubles its intensity and when the whole woodwind section asserts it in D minor, the whole of the strings hurl it back in C minor, both against the solid mass of brass counterpoint, which is climbing out of G minor into B flat. This alternation of wind and strings persists with awe-inspiring effect. Now begins the real clash of opposing forces. One bar after Fig. 34 the side-drum cuts harshly into the music, hammering out its original rhythm without the slightest regard to the tempo of the *Adagio*. The immediate result of this is to drag the music back into F at Fig. 35: the rhythms of the side-drum become freer and more disruptive, but the trumpets combat it with its own weapon (i.e. its own original rhythm) on the dominant of G. The counterpoint in the brass is forced to consolidate itself into harmony, but it flows massively on nevertheless. The side-drum, the very embodiment of frustrated savagery, breaks frenziedly away from all reason in a violent *cadenza*: the composer instructs the player to improvise 'as if at all costs he wants to stop the progress of the orchestra.' But the very fact that this destructive element is given full, anarchic play for its individuality is its own undoing: absolute self-control spells disaster, and desperation is its own victim: the trumpets blare fiercely at their D with increasing urgency, and then the side-drum is swallowed up in a mighty and victorious climax in G major. Not only is it swallowed up; it is forced to contribute to the triumph. With a grandeur that may be quite soberly described as colossal, Nielsen sustains the music on this supreme level for four pages of slow time, with a great striding bass that seems to encompass the whole earth. At Fig. 38 the tumult begins to subside; the side-drum, now powerless but still defiant, tries vainly to assert itself. There is an echo of Ex. 41 in bassoons, and flutes refer to an almost forgotten thing, the triplet figure of the bass first heard before Fig. 22. The music settles to a soft chord of G major. But the victory was hard-won, and the air is full of tragedy; a lonely clarinet sounds a moving *cadenza*, derived from that most meaningful idea in the whole vast movement, Ex. 41, and it has all the tragic significance of a *Last Post*. At the end it dies away over the slowly vanishing rhythm of the side-drum. Who would have thought that so much could have come out of a gently waving viola line that appeared in empty space?

From the ashes and ruins left by the conflict rise the regener-ative energies of man. In this second movement is the answer to Vaughan Williams's sixth Symphony, given twenty-five years in anticipation, and it is a facile argument that puts the responsibility for Vaughan Williams's pessimistic outburst entirely on the atomic bomb. Nielsen's optimism is not of the easy kind; it takes grit—that word perhaps best describes the character of the opening of the second part of the symphony, in a tough-sounding B major-minor, the furthest remove from F. There is a hard-held E in the chord and the bare sinewy sound of the open fourth is prominent:

Ex. 46

The presence of the persistent E makes the key of B unstable and after a sudden silence (immediately following the end of the quotation) the E bursts out, harmonized as the dominant of A, into which key the music drives with Ex. 46(*c*), inverted to an upward leap (four bars after Fig. 40). Six bars later comes a phrase that recalls the style of the finale of *The Inextinguishable* (compare with Ex. 38(*b*)). More strenuous assertions of Ex. 46(*c*), with harmonies that are like the shifting of debris, lead to a fiery treatment of Ex. 46(*a*) and its derivatives in a passage of growing dissonance and tension touching the dominant of E flat. Then the disturbance subsides with the music quite definitely in A major. At Fig. 45 an oboe plays a new theme of calm happiness, as if breathing new, clean air:

Ex. 47

Any attempt to derive this from Ex. 44 is rather too in-genious: if it comes from anywhere, its idea originates in Ex. 46(*d*). The balmy atmosphere it inhabits gives rise to an exhilarating stretch of relaxed athletic music. From the oboe the violins take over the subject (with a beautiful touch of harmony); then it goes into the bass with a graceful running counterpoint above. Four bars after Fig. 47 it comes to the surface again as the dominant of E is felt, and it grows most naturally into Ex. 46(*a*), in a kind of revolving canon. There is a *crescendo*; then a silence: at Fig. 49 instead of the expected E major there comes a sweeping *tutti* (without trombones or drums) which at first has Ex. 46(*a*) in the bass and modulates all round the harmonic world before finally swooping majestically on to the dominant of E flat minor (four bars before Fig. 52); this passage may remind some readers of Brahms, but in its context its essence is deeply opposed to the Brahmsian *ethos*. It runs straight into *staccato* string quavers that avoid E flat and

In the 1920s

eventually settle, *ppp*, on the key of B major, with flute and bassoon giving out a new blend of Ex. 47 and 46(*a*) (page 98 in the score). It looks as if B major is to be reinstated.

This exciting development continues with more woodwind added, interjecting Ex. 47 periodically with strange dissonant harmony, while the strings keep up their racing quavers. The key of B, as before, is not stable; the sound becomes extremely involved as Ex. 46(*a*) and (*b*) join in a labyrinthine whirl that raises the music to boiling-point (*circa* Fig. 57). The bass (the true one is played by bassoons, bass trombone, and tuba) moves into the region of A flat; then at Fig. 58 it tries to restore B, but loses it again, landing itself in the dangerous area of F; at Fig. 59 the upper harmony converges on a chord of D major, and all the clashing lines of counterpoint are suddenly cut off, leaving the strings fiercely attacking an E flat. The strings rise titanic-ally in an effort to return to B, and the music becomes incan-descent. At Fig. 60 the white-hot high B of the strings is then revealed by the entry of Ex. 46(*a*) on the wind to be no longer a tonic, but the dominant of E. Ex. 47 flies by (horns) while the strings sustain the piercing high B. But this passage already passed its peak when the tonic B proved once more unstable, and there is soon an impressive subsidence on to the key of D (Fig. 64). This chord helped to undermine B at Fig. 59. Why?

B is the remotest key from F: it thus represents an intense drive to banish inertia. There is still no reason, now that the first movement's war is over, to suppose that apathy and reaction may not dog those bent on reconstruction. On the contrary, those plagues need to be ceaselessly checked. The first ill omen came in the last passage, before Fig. 59, with streaks of A flat, F, and D. But what does this D major mean now? At Fig. 64 (*poco più mosso*) the strings resume their duple quavers (they have been playing triplets) and the wind bring in Ex. 47 in a plain D major: the vibration goes on, but

H

the music stands still in this key and there is a terrifying sense of impotence as the rhythm deteriorates and repeated Ds begin to sound all too familiar (the mood here is a truly extraordinary anticipation of parts of the second movement of Vaughan Williams's sixth).   The bass slithers down and then the full, grim import of the D major is made clear as the repeated Ds are combined with a chord of A flat.   Here (Fig. 67) are the quicksands of the first movement, discovered with frightening ease.   Was all the struggle useless?

The situation is made even more critical by the fact that the Ds are at once answered by equally definite A flats in the same rhythm.   In the first movement the D had the advantage of being able to flash, isolated, against the dim background of A flat: here the two tones are equally opposed, upon shifting, treacherous harmonic sands.   Neither has any power over the other, and the passage exerts a terrible hypnotic fascination as it becomes more and more evident that nothing can save a catastrophic relapse into F, the mean between the two 'contra-dictory' keys.   This occurs at Fig. 71.   A hapless fugue flutters in F minor:

Ex. 48   **Presto**
1st VLNS. *con sord.*
p

It is violently interrupted at Fig. 77 by the drum and the frenetic shriek of clarinets: it resumes its headlong flight at Fig. 78, trying desperately and unsuccessfully to escape from the key of F.   The more it rushes the more its panic grows, reaching monstrous proportions.   At Fig. 81 a remarkably hectic effect is caused by a close *stretto per arsin et thesin* (the answer being off the beat): the frenzy mounts, but the fugue

remains helplessly rooted to the spot.   The texture threatens
to disintegrate entirely at Fig. 87, but with a furious burst the
full orchestra attempts to tilt itself out of F; it falls exhausted
into D flat, which is only the flat sixth of F minor, and the
terror turns to despair as wailing scraps of melody expire over a
pedal D flat.   What can be done?   The lesson of this fugue
is that panic is futile: only quiet, level-headed thought can solve
such a problem as this.   Very well then, the music has not
really left F; let it think its way out of it with calm concentration
in a slow fugue, using the wisdom and maturity gained from all
the foregoing experience.   So, quite calmly taking F as its
point of departure, another fugue begins, *Andante un poco
tranquillo*, on the following subject, which has an upward
trend that is already vaguely familiar:

Ex. 49   **Andante un poco tranquillo**

Also familiar is the little figure of a dropping fourth that
punctuates its phrases.   The answer comes not in the dominant
but in A flat: the subject itself hesitates between F major and
minor, and A flat is not far away from the latter.   At Fig. 93
the irregularity of this fugue reveals marked purpose; the next
entry of the subject is in E flat.   The cool poise of the counterpoint becomes warmer in feeling and there is a *crescendo*: but the
problem is not solved with ease; E flat is not established in its

own right, for it is but the dominant of A flat.   At Fig. 94
the subject enters in C.   This is still the dominant of F, and at
Fig. 95 a quiet but heavy entry on bassoon and horn weighs the
music down again to that key.   This produces a firm action,
a rise in strength and a genuine modulation to a real C major,
in which the woodwind enter at Fig. 96.   This somewhat
'dialectical' description gives no impression of the profound
and touching poetry of this music; it is Carl Nielsen at his
deepest and most intense, in a vein of searching, sensitive, clear-
sighted thought, informed with generosity and a growing
warmth that come of the fullness of his humanity.   The strings,
their mutes discarded, break in with an uplifted version of
Ex. 47, confirming the key of C by soaring through its dominant, G.   So much achieved by philosophic strength of mind,
it is now time to prepare for the final effort, which must be
physical as well as mental.   With the strong entry of Ex. 47
on clarinets and horns at Fig. 98, the C major darkens to A
minor and there is a tightening feeling of urgency: at Fig. 99
the inevitable happens and the tension is released with a burst
into the original *Allegro* (Ex. 46) which now makes clear that
Ex. 49 was, after all, only a slow version of it.   As before,
the key strives to be B major-minor: the scoring is similar,
except that the melodic line is now strengthened by the
upper woodwind, and at Fig. 100 there comes the same
attack on the dominant of A.   Here is the crux of the whole
matter.

The key of B has always been unstable: one reason for this is
its polar opposition to F.   Its first tendency (because of the
intrusive E in its chord) was to sink to its flat seventh, the calm,
sunny, but relaxed region of A major: this created a sense of
well-being, but it completely undermined any possible establishment of B, despite one huge attempt (Fig. 52 et seq.).   The
reason for this failure is that the key of B cannot, after the long
stretch of A, sound like anything but the supertonic of A if it

is B minor and the 'enhanced dominant' if it is B major.[1]
So B is out of the question as a final tonic, and A is disqualified
by its previous effect (which ended in a disastrous return to F)
as well as by its clear relation of mediant to F. What about G,
the key of the victorious climax of the first movement? This is
philosophically as well as musically not possible, for a similar
reason that the finale of the second Symphony could not appear
in B major: G major was the field of battle, so to speak, and
the second movement very naturally strove to set itself off a
strong major third above this, in B; to return to it would be a
very real anticlimax as well as a moral defeat. In its determination, the finale chose to start at the remotest point from F; its
choice proved unstable by falling to A. What must it do to
shatter this dilemma? There is only one possible solution that
can satisfy all counts. (i) A must at all costs be repudiated, so
its opposite pole must be sought; (ii) the rise of a major third
between the G *major* of the first movement's end and the B
major-minor of the *Allegro* must be justified by another step of
exactly the same kind; (iii) the key of F must be made once and
for all impossible by the selfsame means that rendered B
unstable, i.e. by establishing its flat seventh, so that any further
suggestion of F would sound merely like a supertonic or (if F
major) an 'enhanced dominant' (the dominant of the dominant). One key will satisfy all these requirements—E flat major.
Such a structure as this is profoundly organic (not to mention
its utter originality), and any one who finds it difficult to follow
in musical jargon had better not worry about it; after all, it is
not necessary to be a biologist in order to understand one's
friends, and the power of the music will be more than enough
to convince most hearers, musicians or not.

Two bars before Fig. 102, the expected A major is violently
thrust away: then comes the majestic passage that appeared at

---

[1] It will be recalled that the B did actually become the dominant of E at
Fig. 60, thus confirming itself as an 'enhanced dominant.'

Fig. 49, now reorientated to lead to the dominant of C minor (remember its previous ending on the dominant of E flat minor). C minor is a near relative of E flat major: the exciting, pounding quavers rush in, with incisive repeated notes in the brass. In the fourth bar these repeated notes insist on B flat, the dominant of E flat: Ex. 47 sails exuberantly above on woodwind (Fig. 107), and the end is now only a matter of time. The sound becomes more and more tumultu⁄ ous as Ex. 47 rides on the crest of a veritable tidal wave of foaming quavers in the strings: at Fig. 110 the drum reinforces the dominant B flat, and wind and strings answer each other with cries of fierce triumph, urging each other forward with high impetus. The harmony is harsh, glittering, fit to burst with sheer energy, and at Fig. 113 it snaps all remaining bonds by expanding with the force of a detonation in a vast *allargando* that spreads outwards into a blazing chord of E flat major.

In a work of such complexity and depth as this there are many subtle details that cannot neatly be digested into the body of a readable analysis, and the reader may care to note three small points as a stimulus to further adventures in the score:

(1) In the light of the E flat ending it is possible to go back over the score and find hints of this key in unexpected, yet inevitable places. The C flat scales of the bassoons before Fig. 2, for instance, land on a low B flat that is really the dominant of E flat (the C flat being felt as Neapolitan). At the time this seems a 'harsh, meaningless sound'; but is it, in fact, this? The shadows of coming events are not always recog⁄ nizable, just as C flat does not look like B major on paper, but is really the same key. Just before this passage, too, the bassoons show some sign of a leaning towards E flat (two bars before Fig. 1). Other tendencies towards E flat can be found and they could be listed here were it not for the fact that the reader may take pleasure in finding them himself: one passage he should listen closely to is that beginning four bars before

and ending four bars after Fig. 9. Each case must be carefully weighed, for nothing may be ignored in a work of this calibre; on the other hand, conclusions should not be jumped at.

(2) The melody of Ex. 42 takes as its starting-point (the figure marked (a) in the quotation) the minor third of the initial viola line; but the real subtlety is that the clarinet at the very end of the movement makes a very beautiful blend of Exs. 41 and 42, thus showing that Ex. 42 and all its amazing consequences are intimately derived from the 'sine wave' of the violas.

(3) The instability of the final entry of B major at Fig. 99 is made complete by the preceding A (minor) harmony, so that the B already sounds like an 'enhanced dominant' and is less secure at this stage than it was at the beginning of the movement.

These are merely random points, and the musician will find the work a mine of proofs that for Nielsen, form and content are the same thing. In any art this is perhaps the most important principle of all, and the greatest art provides not only the greatest but also the smallest proofs of it. But what supersedes all matters of detail is the impact of this tremendous symphony, which concentrates within its close-knit length the deepest and most pressing problems of modern man; not only does it express these problems but, unlike most contemporary art, it reveals an attitude of mind that can show the way ahead. If all the above musical analysis has seemed too 'technical' it need not prevent any one from listening to the music itself in all its incandescent grandeur and fearless truthfulness. Perhaps the healthiest comment yet made is that of Eric Blom, in the *Observer*, after the performance in Edinburgh in 1950: '. . . if I had any urge to compose, or any gifts, this, living at the time I do, is the sort of music I should like to write.'

Contemporary works (1921–2): Holst, *The Perfect Fool* and Fugal Overture; Busoni, Toccata (pianoforte), Sonatina No. 6,

Divertimento (flute and orchestra); Schoenberg, Serenade, Op. 26; Vaughan Williams, *A Pastoral Symphony*; Janáček, *Kátja Kabanová*; Stravinsky, *Mavra*; Bax, first Symphony; Honegger, *King David*; Strauss, *Schlagobers*; Prokofiev, *The Love of Three Oranges*; Hindemith, string Quartet No. 3; Milhaud, *Les Euménides*; Bliss, *A Colour Symphony*; Roussel, Symphony No. 1.

CHAPTER VII

THE SIXTH SYMPHONY

(*Sinfonia semplice*)

1924–5

THE next important work after the fifth Symphony was the idyllic wind Quintet, Op. 43; this is discussed more fully in Chapter X, but it is relevant to mention it here, since it carries a step further Nielsen's desire to characterize the separate instruments in his music. In Symphony No. 5 the instrumental timbres are more sharply differentiated than ever before in his work, especially in the first half of the first movement. Like Mahler, but with different purpose and effect, he turned his mind increasingly to the contrapuntal aspect of orchestral writing, eventually regarding the orchestra almost as a large chamber group in this last symphony. In a way that is not quite true of any other great symphonist since Beethoven, each Nielsen symphony is utterly different from the others in the series. Each group of symphonies by Schumann, Brahms, Bruckner, Dvořák, Mahler, Sibelius, and Vaughan Williams (to name no others) has a more obvious uniformity of style (not mood) than the six of Nielsen; Vaughan Williams is perhaps less predictable in style than the others, but even so his manner is more circumscribed and his interests not so wide as the Danish composer's. Vaughan Williams, for instance, makes no further explorations after his fourth Symphony; the rest of his work (even the celebrated sixth) penetrates no new territory. His 'unknown region' (the last movement of No. 6) is a dead planet.[1] Only one other symphonist since Beethoven

---

[1] These remarks should not be misunderstood as an 'attack' on Vaughan Williams: he is great enough to reward attempts to understand him.

showed signs that he might have quested for new worlds even if he had lived to be two hundred—Schubert.   It is characteristic of Nielsen that his last symphony, completed six months after his sixtieth birthday, should be a transitional work.   As such it cannot compare in its entirety with No. 5, but it is frustrating to try to imagine what its first movement might have engendered.

Having achieved in the fifth a profound and precise expression of a philosophy it had taken him all his life to grasp and act upon, his natural inclination must have been to write a more relaxed largescale work in which he could enjoy what he had conquered.   This he actually did in the wind Quintet, one of his happiest works, but he probably wanted also to match the symphony with another, more mellow and gently philosophical, *Sinfonia espansiva*.   That this was indeed the case is shown by a letter he wrote to his daughter Anne Marie Telmányi in August 1924, where he said he was beginning a sixth Symphony, which was to be of 'completely idyllic character'; he remarked that he was going to write with the same simple enjoyment of the pure sound as the old *a capella* composers.   This is clearly the origin of the title *Sinfonia semplice*, which remained even after the symphony had taken another, unforeseen turn.   After it was finished, in December 1925, Nielsen made a statement to Andreas Vinding, of the newspaper *Politiken*, saying that in the new work he had sought to compose for the individual characters of the instruments, that to him 'each instrument is like a person who sleeps, whom I have to wake to life.'   He described how, when he was young, he must have had the same feeling, half formed, for when Grieg commented that he used only a small orchestra, he replied, almost apologetically, that he fought shy of doubling instruments.   He went on to say (to Vinding) that at first he used to compose at the piano and then orchestrate what he had done; the next stage was to write directly into score, and finally:

'I think through the instruments themselves, almost as if I had crept inside them.' After some more remarks about the qualities of various instruments came some cryptic comments on the new symphony:

> I have in my new symphony a piece for small percussion instruments—triangle, glockenspiel, and side-drum—that quarrel, each sticking to his own tastes and liking.[1] Times change. Where is music going? What is permanent? We don't know! This idea is found in my little Humoreske, which is the second movement of the symphony, and in the last movement, a theme with variations, everything is jolly. In the first and third movements there are more serious, problematical things, but as a whole I have tried to make the symphony as lively and gay as possible.

These observations are perhaps not unlike Beethoven's to Schindler, or possibly Vaughan Williams's whimsical programme note for the first performance of his sixth Symphony. But Nielsen's sense of humour was not of the rough Beethovenish kind, and he was as a person so free of sophistication that whatever he said must be treated with care. Notice that he does not say that the symphony is, in fact, cheerful: he simply remarks that he tried to make it so, and though he passes lightly over the 'more serious, problematical things,' these absorb the larger part of the work. The first movement, though it starts harmlessly enough, casts a mighty shadow over the other three (it is by far the biggest in sheer size), and the third movement, *Proposta seria*, is without doubt the most poignant thing he ever wrote. Small wonder that the jollity of the finale is more than tinged with iron. As for the *Humoreske*, its effect is horrifying: the questions Nielsen asks—'Where is music going?' 'What is permanent?'—are no idle postulates for a brains trust; they are urgent, even desperate in view of what he saw and heard around him.

Carl Nielsen was no reactionary and was the last person to

---

[1] The Danish phrase *Smag og Behag* is the equivalent of the French *Chacun à son goût.*

attack experimenters as such: but the 1920s, as every one knows, were infested with 'experimenters' of the most plaguy kind, irresponsible, at bottom hopelessly pessimistic. Although Béla Bartók is far beyond this sphere, Nielsen was somewhat depressed by his question, 'Mr. Nielsen, do you think my music is modern enough?' and afterwards confessed that his opinion of Bartók was rather lowered by this (they met in 1920). The *Humoreske* may perhaps be described as a protest against cynicism by caricaturing the cynics, against triviality by ruthlessly describing it. But the core of the symphony, the first movement, is not spiteful or destructive; there is a deep personal tragedy behind it: Nielsen's heart was showing alarming symptoms of the disease from which he never recovered. This was a hard blow to a man who loved and lived life so vigorously.

Like the fifth, No. 6 has nothing to do with classical sonata form. The first movement is on a gigantic scale and its plan is not describable in conventional terms; even its beginning is not remotely like that of any other symphony ever written; it starts, *tempo giusto*, with four soft Ds on the glockenspiel, introducing a clear, guileless violin phrase (with second violins an octave below):

Ex. 50

Under the held D of the violins a clarinet curls downwards to be joined by a bassoon in liquid semiquavers. The key is G major-minor. Then comes a naïve dancing tune with a trotting oboe and bassoon accompaniment, in feeling not unlike the opening of *Fynsk Foraar* (*Springtime on Fyn*): there is nothing here to suggest that this is no *Sinfonia semplice*:

This unclouded G major soon turns aside, never to return. In the last two bars of page 2 of the score the rhythm of Ex. 51 enters on a B flat and the harmony moves towards the dominant of E flat; five bars before Fig. 1 there is almost a recovery of G, but Ex. 51 begins again in E flat.   Now the air is colder and there is a plaintive little cry (descending demisemiquavers) in the violins.   At Fig. 1 the music closes definitely in E flat with a new idea, containing a figure reminiscent of Ex. 36(b) in the fourth Symphony; in this quotation it is marked (a); and the second half (b) is also very important:

The first real glimpse of tragedy, however, comes nine bars after Fig. 1, with icy harmonies in the woodwind; violas snap out the rhythm of Ex. 51 on E flat, to be answered by second violins on A flat (like dominant and tonic).   The next two bars raise the progression by a minor third, with bassoons and clarinets cutting through with an F sharp.   The two keys A flat and F sharp are of high significance in this movement. Each is a semitone away from G and the tragedy of the great piece is in its fruitless search for the way back to the simple G major; its two points of highest intensity are in F sharp and A flat.   After these disturbing four bars Ex. 51 makes a gallant attempt to dance in at least in E flat: but there is a grim spectre hovering behind it in the form of a portentous slow counter-point on clarinets and bassoons (page 5), and it falters, falling into this rhythmic figure one bar before Fig. 2; there is a *crescendo* and a harsh *ff* banishes simple happiness:

From this point there is a decline and woodwind are left repeating a derivative of Ex. 53 in a cold, cheerless region that turns out to be the dominant of E. Then at Fig. 3 the first violins spring forth unexpectedly with a determined, wiry, very tense fugue subject, in E minor:

Cellos and basses answer in the dominant, with an active counterpoint in the violins, and it looks as if E minor is to be fixed upon. Perhaps there is some hope of reaching G major this way? But the next entry of the subject is in A minor; it causes some growth in tension and the fourth entry restores the balance by refixing E minor. On the half-beat before Fig. 4 the woodwind make as if to start yet another entry, but knit the argument closer by turning it into Ex. 52, in E, with an intense canon, *fortissimo* (at the distance of one bar and the interval of the lower fifth), while the strings slash across with fiery, fragmentary counterpoints. The mood becomes increasingly troubled as the tonal centre shifts to A and then to F: at the start of page 13 in the score the music actually touches G minor, but it is obscured by the dissonant counterpoint, and is passed heedlessly by as a new canon begins on a restless new subject, in which the texture is definitely bitonal, the first entry beginning in C and the second in E:

Ex. 55

Timpani and glockenspiel try to insist on the notes G and D (in the rhythm of Ex. 54), but are sharply contradicted by the E of two muted trumpets, while the canon flows bitterly on in the woodwind.   For the moment the strings have ceased their turbulent commentary, but at Fig. 5, as the woodwind rise again to a *forte*, their interruptions are resumed with redoubled fierceness and strange dynamic contrasts of the most violent kind.   The tension becomes almost intolerable until at Fig. 6 the texture changes abruptly with the sudden silencing of the turmoil on the dominant chord of A flat.   This grim and fantastic music has an awesome effect after the pastoral charm of the opening: on the face of it, these are the sort of grotesque oppositions one expects to find in a composer like Mahler; but there is a profoundly important difference.   Mahler's demoniac passages are largely subjective in origin and expression and one cannot help being caught up in his personal distress when listening to them.   This music has an objective detachment which is rather frightening to some hearers, but is in the end bracing, for it is produced by a fearless mind. Mahler is terrified by what he rightly sees to be destructive in the world and he communicates his fear to the listener.   This is not so with Nielsen, who is able to place the whole of his wide emotional range within the grasp of a larger consciousness: even when he feels forced to express tragic feelings, he is here as much in control of himself as when he is writing the simplest folktune.

At Fig. 6 the involved mesh of lines is cut off for a bare statement, in A flat, of a combination of the subject of Ex. 55 with Ex. 52, stark and intense. The wind join and it seems as if a great contrapuntal paragraph is about to begin in A flat when it is exploded by a hammerblow of the drum and the strings rush furiously in with the vehement fugal matter of Ex. 54. Ex. 52(a) is thrown off by the high woodwind and echoed below in a snarl, and then there comes another abrupt change, this time a passage of marvellous beauty. The fiendish sound ceases all at once and is wonderfully supplanted by a glorious stream of tranquil counterpoint in the purest F sharp major. For the first time since the opening, Ex. 50 is heard, played in augmentation, clear and strong, by the horns; it is now combined with Ex. 52 in beautiful fivepart writing with the startling suddenness of awakening from a nightmare to find oneself gazing into a limitless open sky, breathing clean, sunfilled morning air. There is no parallel to this passage anywhere in music; within a split second the character changes from one extreme to the other. Tragedy is apparently dissolved in flowing counterpoint that might almost have been written 350 years earlier, in spirit if not in technique.

Tovey has pointed to examples of tragic irony in Gluck, Beethoven and Brahms; here is another on the highest plane. Most listeners do not possess what is euphemistically known as 'perfect pitch,' and those who do may be forgiven if they are not sure what key this passage is in when it comes so blindingly out of the chaos. Hearing the first phrase (Ex. 50) again, serene and majestic, they might easily think that this is some sort of recapitulation in G major, dramatically brought about

Family group on the composer's sixtieth birthday

Left to right: Mrs. Irmelin Eggert Møller, Anne Marie Carl Nielsen, Prof. Eggert Møller, Carl Nielsen, his son Hans Børge, Mrs. Anne Marie Telmányi, Maren Telmányi, Emil Telmányi

and 'transfigured.' Now Nielsen does not believe in trans⁄
figurations and this radiantly lovely music is a myth: if it were
real it would be half a tone higher, but it sounds real enough
to make one catch the breath, and its full tragic meaning is
made most movingly clear when its great glow fades into soft
harmonies that become slowly dimmer as the shrill faint sound
of the high piccolo hints ominously at the dotted rhythm of
Ex. 54. Just before the piccolo intrudes, a new idea occurs
which must be quoted (Fig. 8):

The harmony darkens to D minor in twelve bars and then,
beginning in A minor, the woodwind begin a nervous,
chattering *fugato* on Ex. 54. The successive entries are in
strange, irregular keys (G sharp minor, B flat minor, C sharp
minor) and the counterpoints are wry.   In the bar before Fig. 9,
Ex. 50 breaks in on violas in A flat, answered above by Ex. 51
in the next bar: out of these fragments and rhythms a new,
strained contrapuntal web forms.   Four bars before Fig. 10 the
strain becomes unbearable and the texture disrupts into flying
splinters: at Fig. 10 itself the violins are left pouring out a
violent and twisted cataract of notes, and in the second bar
before Fig. 11, Ex. 50, now the very reverse of idyllic, cuts
harshly into it, forcing the music on to a mighty crashing chord
of B flat, with the calm Ex. 56 turned into a fierce flare of
brass.   The tempo is now precipitately increased to *allegro
passionato*, and the chord of B flat is engulfed by dissonance;
a colossal string passage in hurricane⁄like semiquavers races
headlong for the next sixteen bars with alternating entries in
the rest of the orchestra of Exs. 50, 52(b), and 56, each
attack of Ex. 56 intensifying the dissonance.   Then the whole

I

detonates with titanic force, leaving a screaming semitonal discord (C and B) in the high woodwind and muted horns still splitting the air. For all its harshness, this terrific outburst leaves no doubt whatever that the music is now in A flat. The pace is at once reduced to *lento, ma non troppo* and below the high discord may be heard the cold tone of the glockenspiel on E flat: then the violas and cellos, with full force, break out with what seems like an agonized new theme until it turns into a new, very tragic treatment of Ex. 50. Muted trumpets and horns add to its despair (Fig. 13), and it dies away.

The reaction from all this is a remote, high canon in the violins, which takes Ex. 50 as its starting-point, with the glockenspiel still softly echoing the dotted rhythm. The lower strings (without basses) respond *forte*, the cellos merging Ex. 50 with Ex. 52(*b*), and the music gains intensity once more. During this moving passage (before and after Fig. 14) the key of G major is touched twice, with infinite pathos, for it is now a very distant key and is a mere passing inflexion. Slowly the lament mounts as woodwind instruments are added; for all that the music is filled to breaking-point with sadness, it never once loses its dignity, even when the *crescendo* grows more clamorous with a return of the rhythms of Ex. 54. The harmony once again is full of inner strife. For the third and last time, with shattering drum-strokes at irregular intervals, Ex. 54 is heard in the form of a *fugato*, now in A flat. Its initial leaping figure is now increased from an octave to a minor ninth. A clarinet flies wildly in and the horns (two muted and two open) enter with a writhing line that becomes the release for a flow of bitter counterpoint from the woodwind, in the style of the canonic writing earlier in the movement, while the strings unleash a whirlwind (the woodwind counterpoint blends elements of Exs. 50 and 52 with free parts). The drum hurls into the mass of conflicting lines a thunderous A flat, which it holds, and the tumult subsides as if crushed. The whole vast movement dies quietly out with a lonely unharmonized line in A flat minor and major (violins in octaves), that turns Exs. 50 and 52(*a*) into a poignant melody before the bassoons enter, gently guiding the music to its close in A flat major. The very last sound is of the glockenspiel, with the dotted rhythm, and its very last note is E flat, a semitone, so near and yet so far from that with which it so happily began the symphony.

If Nielsen had stopped at the end of this first movement, it would still have stood on its own as one of his most impressive works, a tragic onemovement symphony. Its basic idea, the loss of and fruitless search for a state of childlike joy, is so utterly simple and is expressed with such inexorability and piercing beauty that the work becomes a very real reflection of the times rather than a merely personal screed. It is much more truly 'typical of the age' than all the spineless cacophony that is usually regarded in that 'light.' As always in Nielsen's finest work, form and content are inseparable, and the placing of F sharp and A flat against the G major of the start is one of his simplest and most powerful strokes of genius. For all its tragic force and complex emotions, this movement is, so far as its basic structure is concerned, much more a *Sinfonia semplice* than the first Symphony.

The rest of the sixth Symphony must frankly be faced as a kind of appendix in which Nielsen descends from objectivity to subjectivity: none of it has either the stature or the power of organization of the first movement. In the *Proposta seria* is a pathetic attempt to recover himself, couched in terms of the most heartrending sorrow: after this the 'jollity' of the finale turns to ashes. Between the composition of the first movement and the *Humoreske* he fell into a low state, physically and mentally depressed and exhausted. The first movement was finished on 20th November 1924 and the *Humoreske* was quickly written in January 1925; his courage was so depleted that even the great celebration for his sixtieth birthday could not lift him out of himself, and the whole symphony was not finished until 5th December 1925: as so often, he had to rush to complete it in time for the first performance, which took place only six days later.

It cannot have needed much strength to compose the *Humoreske*, but it gives the appalling impression of having absorbed every ounce of a nearly exhausted resource; it thus has a horrid power. 'Analysis' is scarcely what it requires here, for disorganization is its essence. Full of spasmodic percussion rhythms, spiky melodic lines, and irreconcilable tonal contradictions, it is in the nature of an exasperated attack on stupidity and viciousness; it is evidence that even a great artist can be brought so low as the level of his petty adversaries, though by its very contrast it throws into relief the greatness of his best work. It begins with disjointed fragments from triangle and side-drum, with inarticulate, animal-like sounds from piccolo and bassoon; out of these noises is derived a twisted, ugly subject on a clarinet:

Ex. 57   **Allegretto**

The style is Contemporary Acrid, though this is not twelve-note music; but there is no abiding tonal centre: if this movement were performed under the name of some adherent of the tinpantonal school at a festival of modern music, it would no doubt be hailed as a masterpiece, but Nielsen adopts this manner when he is at his lowest ebb. The desperate confusion increases as the parts 'quarrel.' At Fig. 4 there is a subsidence in the bickering and then comes a new, strutting theme in F sharp major, clarinet accompanied by bassoons:

Ex. 58

cresc. poco a poco

This is almost pathetic (notice that the accompaniment is marked to be louder than the tune), but it is grossly smeared across by a sudden downward *glissando* on a trombone, like a crudely unconcealed yawn of contempt (the composer confirms this in a footnote). The tune limps along and another trombone sneer puts it out of countenance, so that while the clarinet continues in F sharp major, the accompaniment side-slips into D minor. Every time the music shows some faint sign of genuine humanity, the trombone gapes hideously at it, and there are no less than eight of these interruptions. Thematic elements of Exs. 57 and 58 are mixed together, and six bars after Fig. 6 the two clarinets make a short-lived attempt at a sinuous chromatic canon. In the end the movement dissipates itself into the aching void whence it came.

Next comes the *Proposta seria, Adagio.* Its deeply affecting fugue-like beginning in the strings, which have been silent throughout the *Humoreske,* is, despite its tragic feeling, a profound relief after the foregoing vituperative noises. Once more the music is back on a higher plane of thought; the main subject, *molto intensivo,* has extremely characteristic chromatic inflexions that serve only to heighten its faithfulness to one central note:

Ex. 59

This opening suggests that a great slow movement is about to wipe out all memories of the *Humoreske*; the key at first seems to be E minor, but after the third entry of Ex. 59 the sustaining force passes away into perplexed harmonies, above which the second violins cry out with a dissonant A flat. The other lines cease and the second violin line falls helplessly into a chromatic spider's web, where it remains entangled, making continuous struggles to escape. Through this web looms Ex. 59 on the horns in thirds, with the two bassoons imitating it at a different pitch, and the music becomes tonally centreless. In the bar after Fig. 2 it almost makes a veiled cadence into F sharp, but the flute nullifies this with a new theme in A flat minor. This subject, which it is not necessary to quote, is in slow triplet rhythm and begins to creep about contrapuntally between flute, clarinet, and bassoon, until all the violins interrupt vehemently with Ex. 59 on what seems to be the dominant of G. These shadows of F sharp, A flat, and G may be regarded, especially in view of the intense burst of feeling they arouse, as having oblique reference to the first movement. The violins' outburst slips from its key and all the lower strings seize upon Ex. 59, but beginning on the note F, while the violins fall again into the toils of the chromatic web. The bass dips steadily downwards and the intensity slackens again. Once more the flute theme in slow triplets drifts in, with a clarinet in sixths below, at first in F minor, but turning towards A flat. As before, it does not last long, and then a horn plays repeated G flat crotchets as if to begin Ex. 59 again, while the violins creep chromatically above it. The feeling becomes numbed as (one bar after Fig. 4) the tonality floats significantly into B flat minor, with the violins' stirrings growing feebler; the music fades, and anxious questions are posed between the bass and the woodwind. The answer is enigmatic, the slow building up (on Ex. 59) of a complex diatonic chord that contains a soft contradiction of A flat and B flat minor, a wonderful sound, disturbed only by the little rhythmic movement of the theme, like a ripple on the surface of a quiet pool. The bass enters on a low D flat that seems about to turn the music gently into G flat, but the A flats of the violins hold firm, and the low D flat resolves, after all the other parts have vanished, on to a C. So this short piece ends, like the first movement, in A flat, infinitely sad and tender.

It has been shown that, towards its close, the *Proposta seria* leaned to the key of B flat; this was minor because of the note D flat that also belongs to the key of A flat. It is now clear that there is no hope of ever recovering the carefree G major mood of the very start of the symphony: the finale tries to make the best of a bad job by being in B flat major, which is at least related to G through the tonic minor; it is thus a pale substitute for G major, but is the most that can be done under the circumstances. In any case, the symphony has sustained such harsh wounds (the curse-mark of the *Humoreske* is indelible) that any attempt to restore G major would either seem ironical or pass unrecognized. So B flat it must be.

Flutes, oboes, and clarinets rush in where angels fear to tread, with a shrill introductory passage that foreshadows the main theme. This theme is then given out, *Allegretto un poco*, by an unaccompanied bassoon:

Ex. 60

As a theme it is remarkable; as Frede Schandorf Petersen points out, it touches all the twelve tones, but is in no way atonal, being decidedly in B flat major. At first it seems like a simple Danish folk-tune, but its middle section finds the tonality shifting alarmingly. In the variations themselves, this tonal restlessness is allowed to infect the other parts of the theme with the result that, although the finale never really leaves B flat, its hold on it is nervous and easily shaken. The first variation is scored for woodwind alone, and the trend of events is indicated at once by the twisting of its first phrase (see the second oboe part); the general rhythmic outline of the theme, however, is preserved, and there are skittish interruptions. Variation II, *Allegretto quasi andantino*, starts on horns and is scrappily scored, with snarls and sharp *pizzicato* chords in which all the open strings are used. Already there is more than a hint of the *Humoreske's* influence. Variations III, IV, and V bring about a complete change, *più vivo*, with scurrying *pianissimo* triplets on muted strings, like a ghostly scherzo, beginning with first violins alone.   By the end of III, firsts and seconds are together; the tonality is obscured but not ousted and the theme's shape discernible.   Variation IV begins with the entry of the lower strings (the effect is fugue-like) and a quick rise to *fortissimo*; soon the continuous texture is curtly broken up, and loud *staccato* rushing semiquavers show their teeth, and dominate Variation V (*brioso*).   Here the varied theme starts off (behind the semiquavers) as if to develop a long sustained line in thirds in the woodwind; but it is soon chopped into rhythmic pieces: the bass, oddly enough, punctuates this variation with a short downward-thrusting phrase that was used in the original discarded ending to the flute Concerto. Variation V peters angrily out and VI introduces another marked contrast, a little waltz, at first on muted strings.   The harmony sets out to be the simplest imaginable, but subversive elements creep into it and Variations VI and VII are, in fact, a single increasingly hectic treatment of the waltz rhythm, VII beginning with a very rough statement of the first phrase on trombones in square rhythms, answered by wild waltz rhythms from the rest of the orchestra; the whole variation consists of clashing rhythms and keys and culminates in an extremely ferocious outburst.   As this spends itself, trombones, tuba, and drum crash in with a dismal clangour and then the music dies away gloomily on the dominant of B flat minor.   Out of this dimness grows Variation VIII, *Molto adagio*: once more the music tries to rise out of its despondent mockery of gaiety in a deeply pathetic slow movement.   The theme is in the middle register (horn, violas, cellos) at first: while it lasts it is very moving, but there is a slight hastening (*un poco di più*) and the flow of warm blood that seemed to begin is chilled.   Wood-wind destroy the continuity of the texture and the glockenspiel starts a restively monotonous tinkle; there is a *crescendo* to a harsh *fortissimo* and then a slow and hopeless collapse.   Now is the opportunity of Giant Despair; Variation IX is a short and almost lethal noise in the style of the *Humoreske*, in which the only warped remains of melody are to be heard on xylo-phone, tuba, and bassoon, the rest being a tintinnabulation of triangle, side-drum, and bass-drum. All that is now left is a coda, beginning with a bald brass passage marked 'Fanfare.' The side-drum is prominent, and it incites the violins during a feverish *cadenza*-like rush that rouses the whole orchestra to a disruptive outburst; this disintegrates, leaving the last notes of the theme alone on an exposed bassoon. But it is too late for such things to be comic, and there are warring elements until the very end, which comes with abrupt sardonic humour.

Thus ends Carl Nielsen's last symphony, and it is, taken as a whole, bitterly disappointing in more senses than one. But perhaps it is so in only one sense after all, for its artistic short-comings are so clearly the result of its emotional origin that even in its disjointedness it demonstrates Nielsen's instinct to identify form with content. One can be thankful that it represents merely a passing phase; although it is his last word as a symphonist it is by no means his last as a composer. Besides the two fine wind Concertos, in which he recovers his objectivity to the full, there is, above all, his last testament, the great organ work *Commotio*. This is enduring evidence that he regained his strength of mind and clearness of vision. The sixth Symphony will always be a source of controversy and a moving document, but it should never be played where Nielsen's music is not familiar, unless, perhaps, the first move-ment is given by itself; that is capable of standing alone as a magnificent tragic work, rising from the deepest springs of human feeling.

Other works appearing at the time of Nielsen's sixth: Vaughan Williams, *Flos Campi* and Concerto in D minor (violin and strings); Sibelius, Symphony No. 7; Ravel, *L'Enfant et les Sortilèges*; Bloch, Concerto Grosso; Schoenberg, wind Quintet; Prokofiev, second Symphony; Berg, chamber Concerto (pianoforte, violin, thirteen winds); Holst, first Choral Symphony; Stravinsky, Concerto (pianoforte and wind); Malipiero, *Filomela e l'Infatuato*; Casella, *Partita* (pianoforte and orchestra); Bax, second Symphony; Honegger, Concertino (pianoforte and orchestra); Walton, overture, *Portsmouth Point*; Gershwin, piano Concerto.

CHAPTER VIII

THE THREE CONCERTOS
(Violin, Flute, and Clarinet)

THE large classical concerto scheme with *ritornello* was never attempted by Nielsen: very few composers have felt inclined to risk it since Brahms and Dvořák. Elgar's violin Concerto (written about the same time as Nielsen's) attacks the problem, and the first movement of Busoni's enormous piano Concerto, together with Reger's hugely comprehensive works for piano-forte and violin, are perhaps the most important examples of this difficult form since Brahms. Nielsen was never interested in the thought of writing a concerto on the heroic scale; he put into his symphonies most of his weightier substance, and the three concertos are all more intimate in character. Each has its own individual form, and it is significant that the biggest and most imposing work of the three, the violin Concerto, is in many ways the least important.

The violin Concerto was composed in the wake of the *Sinfonia espansiva* and it is, like the symphony, a very genial work, but much more relaxed. Its shape is unusual, two immense slow introductions, each leading to a full-sized quick movement, in the first case a broad *Allegro cavalleresco* and in the second a peaceful final rondo. The tonal plan is, character-istically, a process from one region to another, and the opening *Praeludium* adumbrates the scheme of the whole work by modulating slowly from G minor to D major (the D major at the end of this section is by no means a mere dominant; it is a key in its own right). The mood is ruminative and the con-ception extremely spacious; a full orchestral chord of C minor is firmly treated by the soloist as a subdominant chord and he launches into a rich *cadenza* over sustained pedals. Five bars after letter A, he leads the music poetically into G major, with the following calm phrase appearing in the strings:

Ex. 61

This idea is most sensitively and unaffectedly used, as the *Praeludium* gradually lifts itself, with passing fluctuations in mood, away from G towards D, where it finally settles in an atmosphere of felicitous peace. Then the *Allegro cavalleresco* rouses itself with this frank and sturdy tune in G major:

Ex. 62

entry of Solo

The soloist repeats it in D with a new continuation, and a big sonata-movement develops with a widely variable texture and a broadly optimistic tone. The main idea of the second group is a contrasting tune of flowing quality, in D major (which here sounds almost like a return to the tonic); the quotation gives it as it appears at letter D on the solo violin, so as to show the little Nielsenish figure that becomes very active; it is marked (*a*):

Ex. 63

It is easy to follow the course of this movement, and the *cadenza* comes just before the recapitulation. There is a lively *più presto* at the end, which is decisively in G major, with brilliant fireworks. The second part of the concerto begins *poco adagio*, wandering plaintively round D minor with a theme that starts, probably by accident, with B A C H.

Ex. 64

This section is perhaps the best in the work and it is a good example of how Nielsen can indulge in chromaticism without ever falling into sentimentality. Eight bars before letter D (page 61 in the miniature score) comes a tranquil new subject (unquoted) in A major. This taken over by the cellos in a C sharp minor that turns back to A; then follows a passage of deep mystery (the figure in the bass suggests the trio of Beethoven's seventh Symphony), after which there is a quiet settling on an A major that is more and more clearly recognizable as the dominant of D. The last movement, *Allegretto*

scherzando, is a gently whimsical rondo on a graceful and humorous tune:

Ex. 65

Allegretto scherzando

The form is very simple, though not without subtleties that there is no space to go into here; the episodes are plainly divided off from the rest and the movement should not be expected to provide dazzling excitement. It will, however, bear repetition better than many a more vivid piece.

Considered as a whole, the violin Concerto is not one of Nielsen's finest works; it pales beside the *Sinfonia espansiva,* and many listeners may feel that it contains too many direct reminiscences of other music, that there is a certain easy slickness about some of its strokes. But it has many beautiful things in it, and it is, on the whole, a more deeply felt work than the violin Concerto of Sibelius.

The flute Concerto is a late work, composed in 1926, and is the first major composition after the sixth Symphony. It is a welcome contrast to that bitter music, and was written for the flautist Gilbert Jespersen; it is exquisitely calculated to suit the character of its dedicatee, inclined to fastidious taste and a love of French music, though there is nothing French in this music, and it contains one of Nielsen's deepest and kindliest jokes at the expense of his friend. There are two movements only, and the first spends all its time looking for a key, opening with a discord:

At first D minor seems to be favoured, and this is rather confirmed by what seems like a 'second subject' in F major, a warmly sympathetic tune that likes to curl towards B flat major:

After enough of this theme to make it seem like the orthodox second group of a sonata movement, there comes a dissonant passage, with the marked entry of none other than the flute's *persona ingratissima*,[1] the bass trombone.　This coarse individual spreads himself all over the score with a grotesque and aimless blether, as if looking for something he has never even remembered to forget, while the aristocratic flute expresses its outraged sensibilities.

When the trombone's maundering has come to naught the orchestra gathers itself in a passage of preparation, foreshadowing a new idea that floats out radiantly on the flute in E major; this is one of the loveliest moments in the work, based on a very simple figure that should be remembered:

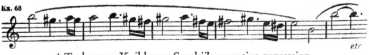

[1] To borrow Kaikhosru Sorabji's evocative expression.

Then the key of E is disturbed and the flute tries to reach it
again in a *cadenza*, but the orchestra contradicts it in a restless
treatment of one of the earlier unquoted themes.   There is
another *cadenza* which the clarinet joins, in a gloomy search for
Ex. 68.   Eventually Ex. 67 enters soothingly in G flat and the
movement ends, pacified but unconvinced, in that key.

The second movement opens impulsively and soon hits on a
charming little melody in G major:

After some subsidiary activity with some more lively matter
comes a new section, a touching, brief *Adagio ma non troppo*, on
an expressive theme heard first on the flute and then in the bass
while the soloist makes beautiful and pathetic comments in
broken rhythms.   Then Ex. 69 returns, again in G major; it
leads, rondo-like, to another new idea, and there is increased
agitation, producing a return of the impulsive thought that
started the movement.   Hard upon this comes the *adagio*
theme again, in the bass below urgent string *tremolandi*; the
reaction from its sombre seriousness is a delicious childlike
version of Ex. 69, *tempo di marcia*, still in G:

K

Now the original ending of the concerto pursued this idea (with another transformation of the theme in dotted rhythm) to a cheerful close in D major, with guffaws of delight from the bass trombone; a happy idea, no doubt, but it missed the real point, which did not occur to the composer until after the first performance. What has the music been searching for all the time? Perhaps it is already obvious to every one that Ex. 69 is only an offshoot of Ex. 68; what is also obvious is that the first movement was hunting for a key, and that its most charmed moments are in E major, with Ex. 68. The second movement found something like the tune, but not its key, and at first Nielsen achieved no more than a jolly ending in the dominant. Then came the brilliant stroke. Why not let the poor old trombone make a real discovery, even if it does give offence to the flute? So the trombone clodhops clumsily in with Ex. 70 in a hopelessly wrong key and, more by luck than judgment (or so it would seem), he lands himself in E major with Ex. 68, adapted to the 6–8 time. This is plainly what everybody has been looking for, and the discomfiture of the flute at having been forestalled by a mere uncouth yokel is clear in the exquisitely graceful and pained phrases he emits. As for the trombone, his chortles of joy take the form of distinctly uncultured *glissandi*, and the concerto ends on this delightful note. How different are these *glissandi* from the dreadful use of the same device in the *Humoreske* of the sixth Symphony! This seems to give the lie direct to that ill-considered outburst.

The flute Concerto is one of the most endearing of all Nielsen's works and its humour is of the profoundest and most sympathetic kind.[1] It represents a throwing-off of his terrible fit of subjective gloom; although his health never recovered, his

---

[1] I most emphatically disagree with the practice of making a small cut in the coda of the second movement; to do this damages the proportions, and even if the composer himself agreed to it (as he may have done on some occasion) he refrained from marking it in the score.

music never again showed signs of disintegration, even in the knotty and often angry clarinet Concerto. Aage Oxenvad was the recipient of this turbulent work, as much intended to suit his temperament and style as is the flute Concerto made for his milder colleague. Nielsen meant to compose a concerto for each of the five wind instruments; he was, alas, prevented: it is not difficult to imagine that if his plan had materialized the five works would have made a unique collection of master-pieces, for no one understood better the individual characters of wind instruments. In the clarinet Concerto choleric humour, pathos and kindliness are mingled in conflict, and the objectivity of the work is shown by the inflexible sense of purpose it conveys. The music has a fractious tendency to change its texture without warning, but this does not indicate pure subjectivity; it may perhaps be regarded as a commentary on the consequences of wilful individualism—subjectivity under observation, in fact. Acting as a sharp spur to the clarinet is an aggressive side-drum part, and the sense of conflict is heightened subtly by the rivalry of two keys, F and E. The concerto has what is, for mature Nielsen, one rare feature: it starts and finishes in the same key; the conflict is such as to prevent the music from leaving its starting point. The opening is firmly in F, with a brittle-seeming, yet formidable theme, *Allegretto un poco*:

Ex. 71

CELLOS & BASSES

mp

The solo enters at Fig. 1, still in F, and then the orchestra, with steely intent, tries to drive home Ex. 71 in E; this E tends

to behave as dominant to A, but there is a fierce rebellion
against it (Fig. 2).   Nine bars later the music is on the edge of
E again, and this is the sort of thing that is constantly taking
place.   F is made firmer by the advent of an apparent 'second
subject' in its dominant, C (Fig. 5), a wistful tune that fails to
sustain a steady *cantabile*.   The first movement conceals beneath
its fitful tempers a stern power, and the side-drum does not allow
it to relax for long.   The recapitulation is heralded by a biting
cadenza in which the strife between F and E is clearly marked;
then bassoons and basses enter on the dominant of F, but the
main theme, Ex. 71, follows instead in E!   Nine bars after
Fig. 8 the cellos and basses make a severe effort to right this;
as a result a violent storm blows up, in which the two keys give
each other no quarter, the clarinet penetrating the harshest
sounds; nor is the side-drum reticent, but Nielsen is very
careful not to overdo this dangerous part.   After this, the
movement dies away, unresolved, with chords of E major
alternating with the dominant of F.   The whole concerto is
continuous, and to divide it into separate movements is no
great help towards grasping it as a whole.   The tempo next
changes to *adagio* with a long, gloomily restless melody on
horn, beginning with a momentary touch of bitonality; C
minor on the horn and E major on the bassoons:

This comparative quiet does not last long, and the side-drum
soon aggravates the music into a wild, strange passage, full of
bizarre strife, the drum growing in force and the clarinet
wailing high against complex rhythms in the strings.   The
passage culminates on the dominant of E before it collapses into

the *adagio* again. After that comes another quick section
(Fig. 20), beginning harmonically in limbo, but with a new
theme emerging on the dominant of E:

Ex. 73

Allegro non troppo

1st VIOLINS

p

It moves immediately to the opposite pole (dominant of
B flat), and becomes increasingly disturbed, and the continuous semiquavers soon form themselves into a rough
sequence out of which the clarinet makes an impressive
drooping phrase, while the bass holds firmly the dominant of
F (Fig. 23):

Ex. 74   SOLO CLARINET

mp espress.

After eight bars the music goes definitely into F, but it flows
without conviction and the same old conflict occurs again from
Fig. 27 onwards, when the dominant of E alternates with F.
At Fig. 29 the *pizzicato* strings make as if to go into E, but a
bassoon enters with a decided new idea in F against them.   F
seems to be gaining the upper hand and the clarinet is left
playing an agitated *cadenza* that leads to a return of the *adagio*
(an unquoted, but most haunting, part of it): this is a profoundly moving passage, almost heartbreaking in its tender
regretfulness, the very essence of Nielsen's most poignant
chromatic style.   It moves towards E, which becomes the

dominant of A, in which key the final section begins with a new theme, almost Mozartian, but with a hard, bare accom/paniment:

Ex. 75 **Allegro vivace**
SOLO CLARINET

The music becomes very fiery and energetic, whipping up a powerful sense of movement as if some real decision were about to be achieved (remember that with Nielsen a decision means the definite victory of a new key). The side/drum, however, continues its disruptive activity and the appearance of Ex. 74 is the first sign of discouragement. The A major turns to minor and eventually, at Fig. 41, the pathetic *adagio* comes again, this time most touchingly stirred by an undercurrent of Ex. 75, which once more tries to set off at its original pace, now on the dominant of E; but it loses its way, and the whole work ends with a quiet inexorable settling down to the key of F. The calm severity of the ending puts the individual conflict into the perspective of a larger understanding: but that conflict has not ceased to exist. One feels that while it has no terrors for Nielsen (since he grasps its meaning), it is the kind of individual struggle that is going on in multitudes of minds that are still groping. The piece cannot therefore be called pessimistic, for while it analyses a personal struggle, it under/lines the fact that such a struggle is the result of self/isolation. There is one interesting fact that confirms the tonal structure already described (the tug of war between F and E): while he was composing the work Nielsen was constantly haunted by a simple, naïve tune in E major, and was undecided whether or not to work it into the concerto.   He eventually wrote to Emil Telmányi, who advised him not to use it; this advice he took, but the effects of this E major idea are shot through the whole concerto.

Of the three concertos the last is the deepest, the second the most lovable, and the first the most spacious.   In the long run it is perhaps the flute Concerto that will achieve the greatest popularity, for it has a ripe sense of fun with a deeply poetic insight into human character; in many ways it is the richest and most original concerto ever written for the flute.   The tense clarinet Concerto, hitting every nail ruthlessly on the head, is tougher matter for most listeners, but the problems it raises will have powerful significance while there is trouble in the world. As for the violin Concerto, its very unusual design is not quite matched by its actual invention, and it may be that the composer had not sufficiently recovered from the effort of producing the third Symphony.[1]   But the three works are all important, and no one writing a history of the concerto can afford to ignore them.

[1] The composer's own comments on the work will be found in Torben Meyer's chapter on p. 199.

CHAPTER IX

LESSER ORCHESTRAL WORKS

As an orchestral composer Nielsen's claim to greatness rests squarely on the symphonies, and most of the works that can be called 'miscellaneous' are not important, though they often show striking characteristics. Like Sibelius, he works at a lower pressure in the smaller orchestral works than in the symphonies; lacking any deep interest in conventional 'programme music,' he found little opportunity of producing large-scale pieces other than symphonies for the orchestra. Thus one finds no great tone-poems to compare with Sibelius's *Pohjola's Daughter* or *Tapiola*: the best of all Nielsen's lesser symphonic works, *Pan and Syrinx*, may perhaps be placed on a level with the Finn's rather neglected smaller masterpiece, *The Oceanides*. To Nielsen all music is in a sense programmatic in that it is a reflection of life, and in speech he always referred to 'so-called' absolute music; but he found that for him music was most accurate in expressing characters or states of mind rather than in illustrating events or actions.[1] None of the symphonies is even remotely related to the Straussian idea of the illustrative tone-poem; none of their titles is generically different from Beethoven's use of the word *Eroica*, and where the music represents a tangible process (as in *The Inextinguishable*) it becomes an artistic analysis rather than a mere description of that process. Thus when Nielsen steps outside the field of critical appraisal into that of pictorialism or simple narrative, he voluntarily and consciously narrows his scope; that is why he could never have conceived a work like *Ein Heldenleben* or the *Symphonia domestica*. His attitude has much more in common with that

[1] See also p. 193 in Torben Meyer's biographical section.

of Berlioz than with that of Strauss: even in the *Symphonie fantastique* Berlioz is far more interested in his hero's states of mind than in baldly describing the imaginary activities resulting from them and when, in *Les Troyens*, he sets about painting a superb picture of the 'Royal Hunt and Storm,' there emerges from it not only an almost living image of nature itself; what is overwhelmingly moving is that all this terrible splendour is seen and felt by Dido and Aeneas, two people caught up in a real, human drama. The same humanity may be felt in Berlioz's masterly treatment of the fête of the Capulets; the more riotously exhilarating the music becomes the more does it illuminate the feelings of the unhappy Romeo. When Nielsen chooses to depict a subject like *Pan and Syrinx* (in which the two characters are not regarded as mythical creatures but as human beings), he is more successful than in his de-scription of the rise and fall of the sun in the overture *Helios*.

Pan and Syrinx: a Nature Scene for Orchestra, Op. 49, was composed in 1918: Nielsen was very fond of Greek mythology and in his browsings came across (in Ovid's *Metamorphoses*) the tale of Pan and Syrinx, which lends itself very naturally to musical representation. There is a note in the score which may be translated as follows:

The goat-footed sylvan deity Pan happens to spy the nymph Syrinx among the satyrs and dryads in the hilly Arcadian forests; he persecutes her with his dances and bleating homage. She, terrified by this fierce wooer, flees to the edge of a forest lake. From here there is no escape left for her, and the gods, taking pity on her, transform her into a reed.

The orchestra is without trombones, but makes use of a variety of percussion instruments: one might expect, perhaps, to find some affinity in this music with Debussy, but there is little of French so-called 'impressionism' in it. The atmo-sphere that Nielsen creates for the small drama is warm and sunlit; one might perhaps say, in meteorological terms, that visibility is very good. The air is certainly not steamy and sub-tropical as in Debussy's *L'Après-midi d'un faune,* nor is it uncompromisingly Nordic, as in *The Oceanides* of Sibelius. The work begins in peaceful pastoral mood, with a softly undulating flute theme over thinly scored string sounds, obviously indi-cating the blissfully unwary Syrinx: the presence of Pan is betrayed by high string *tremolandi,* triangle and tambourine, and the shrill clarinets. Syrinx is at first merely perturbed, but soon is frightened. Every bar is most characteristic of Nielsen, especially in the way his instinct unerringly finds the simplest and most direct way of contriving his effects, while the piece as a whole has a finely graduated sense of climax. Pan tries a great range of devices, from wild outbursts of dithyrambic passion to soft cajoling, and Syrinx's mounting terror culmi-nates in a distraught climax. Then comes the release, and the tone-poem ends magically with a faint and exquisite dissonance in the strings, like the caress of a light breeze blowing softly through a delicate reed on a hushed summer afternoon. *Pan and Syrinx* is an ideal work to play as an interlude (it lasts only eight minutes) in the first half of a concert, between, say, a big overture like *Leonora* No. 3 and a concerto. There are all too few such pieces and one of such exceptional quality as this should prove of great value to conductors who wish to rest the more hackneyed ones in favour of a work that, while it is highly distinguished, offers no difficulties to the ordinary listener.

If one is to treat these lesser orchestral pieces in order of merit the next choice should perhaps be the reflective *Saga-Drøm.* The title is hard to translate into English; it should not be 'dream-legend' for that puts the cart before the horse, and 'legendary dream' seems clumsy. Probably it would be better to call the piece *The Dream of Gunnar,* since it is based on Nielsen's reading of the Icelandic saga in which Gunnar of Hlidarende, exiled and on his melancholy journey to Norway, lies down to sleep; as he sleeps his companions say: 'Now Gunnar dreams—let him have his dream in peace.' It is this sentence that is behind Nielsen's tone-poem, which is ten years earlier than *Pan and Syrinx*, having been written in 1907–8, at a time when he had much free time for reading and relaxed thought. The piece in no way resembles Sibelius's early *En Saga*, which is dramatic and active; all the inner movement of this little work is contained within the outwardly static, poised world of dreams. Emerging from the depths with a shadowy theme, *Andante tranquillo*, a misty chorale tries to form: then it gives way to a soft, disturbed *fugato* that rises to a quiet climax, with the still half formed chorale on the subdued brass against the *fugato* rhythm in the strings. After this comes a more fanciful middle section, with wandering woodwind lines upon a restless *pizzicato* accompaniment, ending in an elaborate *cadenza* in which all the voices of nature seem to commune soothingly together; here the separate players are given only their points of entry by the conductor and are left otherwise free (provided they keep to the main *tempo*). This passage hints at the technique of the remarkable market-scene in the *Aladdin* music (1918), where four orchestras play simul-taneously in four different *tempi*, suggesting marvellously the clashing colours, movements and sounds of an Eastern market-place. This *cadenza* is, of course, much simpler, and it leads to a return of the chorale, which now achieves a tranquil and shapely beauty as the steady rhythm of the *fugato* theme gently enlivens its lovely, iridescent harmonies. In its quiet way this final section, falling into a deeper sleep at the end, is absolutely inimitable. At first hearing the work may sound somewhat baffling, even naïve, but its still, spellbound poetry soon reveals itself.

This is perhaps the place to mention another specifically Nordic piece, the little occasional overture of 1927, called *An Imaginary Trip to the Faroes*, written 'to order' as welcome to some Faroese visitors to Denmark. It is unimportant (the composer himself described it as 'only a piece of jobbery') but it is refreshing; its transition from a mysterious beginning to a cheerful jaunt is imaginatively done, and the traveller lands to the jolly strains of a Faroese folk-song very popular in Denmark, *Paaskeklokken kimed' mildt (Easter bells chime softly)*. Another overture generally thought to be more outstanding is the early descriptive work, *Helios*, in which the sun's journey across the heavens is depicted. This was composed in 1903, when Nielsen and his wife visited Greece, staying in a room that overlooked the Aegean Sea. Its plan is very simple, as one expects, a great *crescendo-diminuendo*, rising from the darkness in C to a central climax in E, and falling back again. The opening, with its deep pedals, its wonderful hushed horn calls, and the gradual glimmering of light, is magnificent: as the key of E is approached, however, Nielsen's inspiration does not quite fulfil its promise, for the climax itself is beset with rather conventional trumpet fanfares and its melodic invention is inclined to be threadbare. Perhaps it was a fundamental mistake (uncharacteristic of Nielsen, who is always so acutely observant) to change the *tempo* at all in the work. The middle section is an *Allegro ma non troppo* (the piece begins and ends *Andante tranquillo*), and this unpoetic as well as unscientific haste as the sun approaches its zenith robs the whole conception of majesty, and what might have been one of the finest of his earlier creations misses its mark. The quick section has, however, some moments of brisk vigour (notably a scintillating *fugato*), and the final return to the shadows is beautifully contrived. If the overture had been a noble and serene slow movement (constructed on the lines of the *Lohengrin* prelude, but with a very different atmosphere!) it would have been infinitely more powerful; as it is, it needs a very fine performance to make it convincing as a whole. It is regrettable that Nielsen left no great concert overtures that can be compared with the symphonies: he was often side-tracked by people who presumed on his kindness, and his dislike of saying 'no' to any one often led him to spend on trifles time and energy he might have used on more valuable things. Nothing could be more frustrating than to try to imagine what kind of overture he might have written (in the period, say, between the fourth and fifth Sym, phonies) to Shakespeare's *Hamlet,* or on the subject of Chaucer's *Troilus and Criseyde.* It is certain that he would have written no overtures to unwritten tragedies, and it is possible that the shrewd, earthy strength of Chaucer's poetry would have appealed to him greatly. One could not imagine him sitting down to write *in vacuo* a 'Comedy Overture' in the manner of Reger or Busoni; he would have needed to define its origin in some living experience or, perhaps, in a play of Aristophanes. As it is, the only humorous overture he left is that to *Maskarade,* a breezy piece, certainly, but not of his finest vintage.

Among the independent orchestral works there remains to be mentioned the very first of them all, his Op. 1, the *Little Suite,* for strings, composed in 1888. This is a remarkably accom, plished piece of work and it is not surprising to know that it was preceded by a good deal of (unpublished) chamber music for strings. The suite is deservedly popular and, early as it is, it already shows a marked individuality, especially in its broad and spacious finale. Very well loved is its delightful middle movement, a graceful and often exquisitely worked waltz, which shows the elegant spontaneity with which he could already manipulate counterpoint.[1]

There is no space to discuss here Carl Nielsen's contributions to incidental music for the stage: the most important are the scores he wrote for Oehlenschlæger's *Aladdin* and for Helge Rode's patriotic piece *Moderen (The Mother).* The market, scene from the former has already been mentioned; it is without

---

[1] There are a couple of other small pieces for strings, the short and somewhat Grieg-like *Andante lamentoso (At the bier of a young artist)* (1910) and a trifle from 1928, a paraphrase of Bohemian and Danish folk-tunes. The former is a poignant piece, but rather too subjective and romantic in feeling to be really characteristic of Nielsen.

doubt the most striking and original part of the music, in which Nielsen is completely successful in capturing a convincing oriental atmosphere. He must have learned much from his travels in the Middle East. Some of it is not very interesting (the rather commonplace *Negro Dance*, for instance), but most is intensely perceptive and colourful. The music for *Moderen* is the other extreme—genuinely Danish, born out of the open fields and fresh air and the simple strength of the peasantry.

CHAPTER X

THE CHAMBER MUSIC

BY virtue of his exceptional contrapuntal gifts Nielsen was frequently drawn towards chamber music; the four string quartets, for instance, written between 1888 and 1906, might easily have begun a series second to none in the music of his generation. His contemporaries, Mahler, Sibelius, Strauss, Debussy, Elgar, for various reasons, had little inclination to write chamber music systematically; even Debussy, when he wanted to turn to large-scale forms, nearly always found the orchestra best suited to his illustrative needs, and Sibelius's insistence on 'cold water' was not so ardent as to drive him to the string quartet as a habit. Elgar's latter-day retreat into chamber music was in the nature of a starvation cure for a long-sated appetite. Nielsen's younger contemporaries, Reger, Holst, Schoenberg: these were more interested in small combinations of instruments for their own sakes. Vaughan Williams is a different case; his tendency towards a reflective looseness of form and texture has always made chamber music foreign territory to him, and when he concentrates powerfully on achieving a high degree of density and terseness of utterance (as in the fourth Symphony), nothing less than the white-hot glare of the full orchestra can express the sense of fierce effort involved: his chamber works are all of a relaxed kind, and may not be counted among his most significant. Nielsen was never inclined towards looseness of structure, nor towards rhapsody, so it is understandable that his first love was the revealing discipline of the string quartet: that he abandoned it in the last twenty-five years of his life is a sad pity, not easily explained. Thus his string quartets are all relatively early works, the last between the second and third Symphonies and belonging to the same year as *Maskarade*, separated from its predecessor by eight years.

There are six string quartets by Nielsen, two of which are mere student efforts, unpublished and of no intrinsic value. The published order of the others is misleading, the F minor, Op. 5, being later than the G minor, Op. 13. As may be seen from the chronological list of works, Nielsen's opus numbers are chaotic and there are not only some works without numbers, but also numbers without works! The composer himself made little attempt to document his output, and when his publishers asked him for an authorized opus number for the particular work in hand he very often was unable to remember how far he had got last time. Conse-quently some numbers were accidentally left out (for readers' information, there are no Opp. 15, 20, 22, 23, 25, 26, 28, 30, 31, 36, 37, 38, 46, 56, so the sooner the other numbers are dropped the better; it would be far more useful to make a habit of giving the year of completion after the title of each work).

The first of the published quartets is that in G minor (1888): as an endeavour it is much more ambitious than the *Little Suite* for string orchestra, composed in the same year; but it is not so accomplished, even after its later revision for publication in 1900. The influence of Svendsen and Brahms is very prominent: there are some individual touches (the cadence at the end of the opening sentence occurs again in the first Sym-phony at a similar place), but the forms are not knit maturely together. The first movement, for instance, has many lively and deft touches, including a very effective *pianissimo* ending, but its changing textures do not flow organically into each other; they lie side by side. The slow movement is rather conventional and the least attractive of the four, and the scherzo is of a kind that Nielsen eventually recognized not to be his *métier*, quick and rather Schumannesque; also

Schumannesque is the trio, much more imaginative. The finale suffers from the faults of most immature last movements, and it attempts, but fails to digest, what Nielsen calls a *résumé*, a coda combining themes from the first, third, and last movements.

The F minor Quartet of 1890 is a definite advance and the composer knew what he was doing when he preferred to release it, rather than the G minor, as his first published string Quartet. Its beginning has already the typical Nielsen sweep and is cogently worked: the material, though it is still Brahmsian, is much more personal than in Op. 13. The first movement has considerable tension and weight. As before, the slow movement is the least successful; he is not yet equal to the taxing task of writing really searching slow music for a quartet, and is often overawed into commonplace. In the third movement, *Allegretto scherzando*, Svendsen helps to give Brahms a Scandinavian air, and the finale, though it has sturdy rustic energy, is inclined to be rhythmically a little stiff. The first movement is without doubt the best part of this work.

A gap of eight years, during which Nielsen wrote the first Symphony, the *Symphonic Suite* for piano, the A major violin Sonata, and the *Hymnus amoris*, separates the F minor from the next string Quartet, No. 3 in E flat (1898). As one would expect, it is a very different matter; compared with this spacious work, the other two quartets are mere tentative exercises. The magnificent first movement, thronged with festive sounds, has an elaboration that brings Reger to mind, especially in some of its apparently wayward chromaticism: but where Reger's sense of movement seems somewhat handicapped by his love of proceeding by fits and starts (the first movement of his powerful E flat Quartet, Op. 109, for instance, has an ebb and flow so marked as almost to be called a stopping and starting), Nielsen welds the whole into a single sweep. One feature of the entire work is uncharacteristic; its determined insistence on its tonic,

E flat. The resulting sense of solidity is perhaps not quite matched by the variety so needed by a work of these dimensions, but there is from the outset that unmistakable mastery with which a great composer makes his presence felt. That the opening movement has the noble effrontery to behave like a sonata rondo is a sign of its self-confidence: the writing is full of those kinds of unobtrusive boldnesses that fill Beethoven's last quartets, and the second group has a floating purity of sound that takes the imagination either back to the sixteenth century or forward to the style of Michael Tippett's F sharp Quartet. The permeating E flat tonality is a constant reminder of Beet-hoven's mighty Op. 127. This movement, even more than any part of the beautiful F major Quartet, is some indication of the heights to which Nielsen might have brought the string quartet in the twentieth century; listening to it, it is hard to believe that it was composed three years before the second Symphony, and it shows clearly that, had he pursued the path it indicates, he could have been the only composer to follow up seriously a line that was cut off with Beethoven's late quartets. That he did not do so is a thing for which (in spite of boundless gratitude for other riches) it is difficult to forgive him. The *Andante sostenuto*, trying to begin at the remotest pole from E flat (A major), falls in a brief but moving intro-duction back to E flat; it more than makes up for the pale, slow movements of the first two quartets, being a superb sustained elegy almost on a level with the *Andante malincolico* in Symphony No. 2; in this case, however, an active middle section creates a fine and purposeful central climax, after which the opening theme returns on the cello beneath a lovely flowing triplet accompaniment; there is a deeply felt viola solo at the end. Next comes a delightful *Allegretto pastorale*, in C major (the key of the climax of the *Andante*), with a brilliant *presto* section in the middle, like all the finest village fiddlers on earth. The peasant-like feeling informs the whole of the finale, *Allegro coraggioso*, less imaginative than the rest of the work, but stretching itself with a lazy strength that should never be under-estimated; but it is perhaps not the finale demanded by the rest.

Another ten years elapsed between the E flat and F major Quartets. In every way the F major (1906) is the most perfect and original of all four: it was at first numbered Op. 19, but later revised and issued as Op. 44. In its first version it had a title, *Piacevolezza*, but this was discarded, together with the designation of the first movement, *Allegro piacevolo ed indolente*, which now stands simply as *Allegro non tanto e comodo*. The 'indolence' of this piece (in reality a watchful and poetic restfulness) is typified by the delicate, seemingly casual way its first theme slips away from the key in its second bar; the move-ment maintains gracious swaying curves throughout, losing not an atom of virility in the process, and embracing a wide range of feeling. The second group is placed in the deep-hued key of C sharp minor (= D flat minor) and, like that of the E flat Quartet, this first movement calmly takes the shape of a sonata rondo; the tonal freedom makes it necessary to reaffirm F major at the start of the development. Its gentle close is followed by a fine slow movement, based on a plain chorale with Aeolian leanings, treated contrapuntally and interspersed with intenser declamatory music; the key is C major, but its tendency towards A minor results in the third movement, *Allegretto moderato ed innocente*, being in that key. This is a charmingly individual, mainly smooth-flowing piece, but with sudden bursts of humour that recall the *Allegretto* of Beethoven's eighth Symphony. The finale belongs to the world of *Maskarade*, gay, graceful, and unpredictable. Altogether this quartet is one of the most beautifully polished of Nielsen's works, and there is much depth behind its smiling charm, a depth that is opened fully in the slow movement. Yet, some-how, it would be going too far to say that it fulfils the promise of the E flat Quartet; it is not a great work, despite its beauty, and one feels justified in expecting greatness: it gives the impression of being a blessed respite in the heart of a great series of works. But that series never materialized, and Nielsen put his full strength into the third, fourth, and fifth Symphonies. Perhaps only a Beethoven could have achieved both.

The only other chamber work for strings that Nielsen thought worth publishing is the G major string Quintet of 1888. This is contemporary and comparable with the G minor Quartet, and is too much under Svendsen's shadow to be of any deep interest; there are already some 'fingerprints' (repeated notes, flattened sevenths, typical cadences, and the like), but there is little that he did not turn to better account later. Amongst the chamber music for strings should also be included the two very original pieces for solo violin, both fully mature, *Prelude and Theme with Variations* (1923) and *Preludio e Presto* (1928). The first performance of the former was given by Telmányi in London, when he and Nielsen were on a visit (the same during which Nielsen conducted the fourth Symphony at Queen's Hall): Telmányi was to give a recital at Aeolian Hall; he was not happy about the final variation, and the composer obligingly rewrote it for him in the hotel, four days before the performance. It was a decided success, and it is surprising that more violinists have not discovered the work. Based on an original tune that is the very essence of all that is Danish, the Variations are extraordinarily resourceful and imaginative, while the Prelude is a masterly example of the art of florid yet disciplined writing. In 1928 the prominent Danish violinist and composer, Fini Henriques, celebrated his sixtieth birthday, and various notabilities contributed to a congratulatory column in the newspaper *Politiken*. Nielsen's contribution was a fragment of solo violin music, thrown off lightly, stopping in mid career. Telmányi saw it in the paper and was so delighted with it that he begged Nielsen to finish it. Although the work is mainly a virtuoso piece (it is no joke for the player), it has a fiery poetry that makes it well worth playing; it is necessary to use a special mute attached to the strings above the bridge, so that the left hand can slip it into place while the bow continues to play on the open strings. The *Preludio* is long and volatile and the *Presto*, vigorously angular, resolves itself into a little tune that recalls the end of the flute Concerto before returning to its fireworks. Both move ments make conspicuous use of whole tone progressions in a very individual way.

The two sonatas for violin and piano are both of great value, the one representing Nielsen at his youthful best (1895) and the other (1912) showing the first sign of the toughening fibre that was to produce *The Inextinguishable* and the fifth Symphony. The first, in A major (Op. 9) is a clean, trenchant, glowing work in the Brahmsian tradition, but with many evidences of strong personality: the first movement is marked, characteristic ally, *Allegro glorioso*, and glorious it often is. It is fascinating to hear many of Brahms's figures of speech, stripped of all traces of romanticism and filled with a young countryman's fire; the real attractiveness of Nielsen's first period is in the way in which he is able to learn all the techniques of his romantic predecessors and to illuminate them in a fresh, inimitably clear light. The *Andante* of the A major Sonata is a lovable example of this; outwardly Brahmsian, it is inwardly and serenely Danish. So is the swinging, carefree finale, whose main tune anticipates that of the Phlegmatic Temperament in its rhythm and the *Sin fonia espansiva* in its spirit. The second Sonata is quite another question: here is a new voice; after the sunny period of the *Espansiva* and the violin Concerto comes a note of disturbance. This work is usually said to be in G minor, but that key is about the only one that never appears in it. The first movement has the signature of two flats, but its real key is E flat (in so far as it can be said to assert a key); the opening phrase on the violin certainly might appear to be in G minor if one ignores the piano part, but the harmony definitely places it in E flat. The movement has the queer marking of *Allegro con tiepidezza*; its beginning is quite tepid, but it is not long before boiling-point is reached. The tonality is extremely restless and only a detailed analysis could trace its course: there is one remarkable anticipation of *The Inextinguishable* in the middle of the develop-ment, a harsh *crescendo* in which the violin double-stops, with a trill on B and C sharp and a screaming high C sharp above it, while a Beethovenish bass growls and thunders in the piano; this looks forward to the fierce *crescendo* at exactly the same corresponding place in the first movement of the symphony. At the end this piece subsides into a cold, numbed E flat again. The slow movement is wonderfully broad, in character heroic and tender by turns, in B minor (= C flat minor), and its coda is one of the most touching pages in Nielsen's music. Third and last is an *Allegro piacevole* that belies its name by the irregularity of its rhythms and the mobility of its tonality: the key signature returns to two flats, and the key is at first definitely B flat. The movement is a kind of rondo in swinging waltz rhythm; the theme starts in B flat but is soon in B major without the slightest trouble; its next entry is in A and it finally settles in C, a key that Nielsen took much pains to establish firmly at the end of the exposition in the first movement. This C major is so firmly fixed that it successfully withstands a furious assault by the piano, which hammers out a rapid succession of B flats. By now Nielsen's use of the flat seventh can be taken completely for granted. This sonata is a knotty work that repays the closest study; English listeners do not find it easy to grasp, but to persevere with it is to discover a disturbing but profoundly healthy experience.

Lastly in this chapter must come the chamber music with wind instruments. In this field Nielsen wrote one very important work, one smaller piece, and one that may definitely be called a trifle. The trifle is the little pair of pieces for oboe

and piano (Op. 2) of 1889, a *Romance* and *Humoreske,* very
engaging and also typical, but insignificant.   In 1914 he was
asked to write a small work for an odd combination, clarinet,
bassoon, horn, cello, and double-bass, and he responded with a
delightfully humorous piece called *Serenata in vano.*   It has a
real rustic charm and the opening section suggests a warming-
up process in readiness for the serenade; then comes a lovely,
persuasive slow part, all moonlight and whispers: but it avails
nothing, and the little band slouches off, trying to keep its
dignity in a ridiculous *tempo di marcia*, disconsolate, prosaic,
and not too well in step.

After the herculean labours on the fifth Symphony came the
need for relaxation, and while that mighty work was yet
unfinished, he began the delectable wind Quintet (1921–2).
The idea came when he heard the Copenhagen Wind Quintet
rehearsing Mozart; the players were Paul Hagemann (flute),
Svend Chr. Felumb (oboe), Aage Oxenvad (clarinet), Hans
Sørensen (horn), and Knud Lassen (bassoon).   Hagemann
was later replaced by Gilbert Jespersen, for whom the flute
Concerto was composed.   All these players became his
personal friends and the work is written with an intimate
understanding of their individual personalities; in the final
variations each player is given a prominent passage that
typifies himself as well as his instrument.   It is not surprising
that Mozart was the cause of this work, for it has the true
Mozartian grace and clarity; there is also an open-hearted
humour that suggests Haydn.   Yet it is in his maturest style,
completely Danish in feeling, full of subtle originality.   The
first movement is in E, but has strong leanings to A, in which
key the remaining two movements fall.   It is a great pity to
omit the repeat in the *Allegro ben moderato*, for one thereby not
only loses ten bars, but also robs the start of the development
of some of its freshness.   The piece is full of pastoral and forest
sounds.   The second movement is a lazily comic minuet,

with long stretches of unashamed two-part writing, and a mischievous trio. The finale (a theme with variations) is prefaced by a long *Praeludium*, in which the oboist changes to cor anglais; this is the deepest part of the Quintet, the most bare kind of nature-music, returning for a moment to the wild sounds of some of the fifth Symphony. But it fades, and the last movement begins with a gentle tune that is taken from Nielsen's own *Hymns and Sacred Songs* of 1912–16 ('My Jesus, make my heart to love Thee').[1] There is no religious significance in his choice of this chorale; it is typically Scandinavian, cool and clear, and admirably suited for variations, of which there are eleven. They range from calm reflection to grotesque humour (the funniest is the fifth, a dialogue between an irascible clarinet and an infuriatingly imperturbable bassoon), and at the end the chorale returns in a new, plainer guise, as if to disclaim its connection with such frivolity; it is now marked, with delicious humour, *Andantino festivo*. In this kindly mood Nielsen bids farewell to chamber music altogether; the wind Quintet is one of his most popular works and will always remain so. It is a profoundly sympathetic confirmation of the humanism he fought to establish in the fifth Symphony.

---

[1] This is a very bad translation of *Min Jesus, lad min Hjerte faa en saadan Smag paa dig*: *Smag* means, literally, 'taste.' There is no way of rendering this line accurately in convincing English.

CHAPTER XI

THE KEYBOARD MUSIC

NIELSEN did not begin to compose seriously for the piano until 1916. He was not a brilliant pianist, and this fact has inevitably led to criticisms of his style of writing for the instru‑ment. Among critics, pianoforte style is still a vexed question, and it may be useful to touch on it in a general way before considering particular works. Luckily, the old prejudices are now dissolving; one does not often meet that peculiarly blinkered outlook that condemns all piano writing not rooted in Chopin, Liszt, or Schumann. Such writing used to be called, automatically, 'unpianistic.' Now, of course, it is more widely recognized that, in any medium, technique is not a matter of orthodoxy, but a matter of imagination. What 'comes off' is what the composer has truly imagined, for the ability to write expressively and brilliantly for an instrument does not altogether depend on a close study of its technique; it comes rather from a vividly imaginative appreciation of its character. It is a good maxim in composition that if a com‑poser genuinely imagines what he writes, it will be playable, even though it may present difficulties, and any modifications it demands in the instrument's structure will be possible ones. Unplayable music is not unwritable; but it is quite unimagin‑able.

The character of an instrument depends, of course, on the temper of the times; the piano is perhaps the most adaptable of all instruments—it can effectively produce sounds ranging from the most meltingly Debussian soft iridescence to the ferocious percussiveness of Bartók, to say nothing of Henry Cowell's 'tone‑clusters.' Even its oft‑cited inability to sustain has been

exaggerated and can in any case be used positively; in Beethoven's late piano works, for instance, his use of long, slow
sentences, melodies, or successions of chords (the most wonderful example of the last being Variation XX in the Diabelli
set) has been widely misunderstood. Too often has it been
thought that such passages would be the better for orchestration,
to give them 'continuity of sound': this idea misses the vital
fact that Beethoven actually gains a higher degree of continuity
by relying on the evanescence of each note to create new tension
before the next impinges. Of all the great masters none
has been so persistently and blindly accused of 'unpianistic'
writing as Beethoven and Schubert. Beethoven's style, especially, has been misunderstood by the romantics, so much
so that no one has properly followed it up (any more than any
one has had the courage to accept the implications of the late
quartets). His keyboard writing is often bare, harsh, even
gruff compared with Schumann's or Chopin's; but it must be
compared, not with these, but with Mozart's, Haydn's,
Dussek's, and the styles from which it grew.[1] This would not
be the place to go into its details, but the question has been
raised to point home the fact that the enjoyment of Nielsen's
best piano music depends on the same kind of understanding
that must be brought to bear on Beethoven's. It is not on the
same plane but it accepts the same facts as its basis.

[1] The comparison does not, of course, make it less brusque, but removes
the deposits of nineteenth-century prejudice; nor need one be fettered by the
limitations of Beethoven's contemporaries. As soon as it is seen that everything
Beethoven writes for the piano is genuinely imagined, his consistent purposes
are made plain: his late manner is not so much a style as an inexhaustible
appreciation of the instrument's capabilities. Nearly all other composers have
developed personal, exhaustible styles, that momentarily fix themselves as
norms, while Beethoven's all-embracing treatment is fearfully passed over as
'a bad model for students,' as if it were the work of some awesome eccentric.
The reverse is true; it is the others who are limited to personal mannerisms.
It may be that Beethoven, having been shunned in the nineteenth, may yet found
a pianoforte style in the late twentieth century.

Nielsen wrote some sad nonsense about Beethoven in his little book *Living Music* (that Beethoven vainly attempted to blend the fugal art of Bach and Handel with his own style, that his music generally lacks plasticity and—*currente calamo*—that his art is subjective): in the same essay he shows his enormous respect and love for this composer. The best of men make blunders, and it is one of art's jokes that an artist often tends to be unreasonably critical of the things that influence him most deeply; Beethoven himself gave an example in his remarks about Haydn.

The earliest piano music of Nielsen is trifling, the five small pieces of Op. 3; although there are charmingly individual touches, there is little to suggest that the composer would ever write distinctively for the piano. These date from 1890, but in four years came a much more impressive effort, the *Symphonic Suite*, Op. 8: this is a solid and massive piece of work, which may well interest those pianists who feel some dissatisfaction with Brahms's piano sonatas. Its style owes a good deal to Brahms (and rather less to Schumann, a composer whom Nielsen also gave less than his due), but the writing is more economical than Brahms's early keyboard work. There is quite as much of Nielsen's personality in the music as in the first Symphony, and the opening *Intonation* is a fine, sonorous sound; there are four well-contrasted movements and the finale adopts the procedure of the early G minor Quartet, with a *résumé* of the previous movements, much more successful than in the Quartet. To go into the details of this suite is to make the first sentence of this chapter seem a little hard, but the later works put matters once more into the proper perspective. In 1897 came the amusing but unimportant *Humoreske-Bagatelles* and in 1899 a chip from the bench, the *Festpræludium*.

Then there is a long gap until 1916, when suddenly Nielsen's imagination catches the piano in its grip. In this year he wrote two remarkable works, the *Chaconne* and the *Theme with*

Variations. Both these pieces achieve what he asserted to be impossible—a blend of a Bach-like contrapuntal feeling with a powerful dramatic impulse; the very elements, in fact, that brace Beethoven's last sonatas. Although this music sounds nothing like Beethoven's, it is astonishing to examine the texture and find that Beethoven is almost the only composer who anticipates some of its effects. The *Chaconne* opens in an almost archaic style, and its bare bones are gradually clothed with flesh and blood as it goes on; the theme is like some ancient *canto fermo* and there are twenty variations, the last of which initiates a beautiful soft coda with tranquil rippling demisemiquavers. The key of the whole is D minor (major at the end), and the work covers a wide range of style and feeling, from very powerful brilliance to searching quietude.

The *Theme with Variations* is even more impressive. Its principle is unusual; the theme modulates from B minor to G minor, thus compelling all the fifteen variations to do the same, the last finding its way back to B major in a short, quiet coda. Apart from this characteristic, the theme itself is of the utmost simplicity, a kind of chorale with plain but telling harmonies. Again the range of mood and texture is extremely wide; always the sound is clear-cut, precisely imagined, the harmony subtle but never vague, the counterpoint transparent and intensely characteristic. Sometimes the writing is in bare two-part counterpoint (as in the wonderful decorative canon of Variation III), sometimes in complex and abruptly variable textures (as in the fierce Variation IV), sometimes deeply contemplative (as in Variations VII and VIII, the heart of the work). There is a finely arched growth to a truly astounding climax that is like nothing else than a mighty iceberg, glittering and sparkling in the sun; this is a really new pianoforte style of startling power and grandeur.

Three years later he returned to the piano, and wrote for Artur Schnabel the amazing Suite, Op. 45. This is one of his most striking works; his original intention was to call it *Suite luciferique*, but he afterwards felt that this title might be misleading, though it does hint at the formidable character of the work. There are six movements, throughout which some inimical, yet in the end bracing, force seems to be at Nielsen's elbow. There are two main tonalities, F sharp and B flat, the latter gradually supplanting the former and its satellites: this suite comes between the fourth and fifth Symphonies, and has something of their strength. It begins innocuously in F sharp minor, *Allegretto un pochettino*, but the first movement soon storms into a central climax in B flat, then returning to the opening mood, ending with a questioning air on the dominant of F sharp. The second movement, *Poco moderato*, is short, silvery, icy; at first, influenced by the previous climax, it starts in B flat minor, but it slips from key to key, eventually settling on a chord of G and vanishing. The most profound part of the whole work is the next movement, *Molto adagio e patetico*, one of Nielsen's finest inspirations, a kind of massive improvisation; it begins with strong, impassioned *fortissimo* phrases, seeking B flat from the initial G minor. For all its shortness and apparently rhapsodic form, this piece wields an extraordinary power that makes its quiet moments little short of awe-inspiring; at last it really finds B flat, where it closes softly and most movingly, with anxious, hovering harmonies. The fourth movement contradicts it directly with the plainest F sharp major, *Allegretto innocente*, which, however, unconsciously betrays its insecurity by making its first move to its subdominant; but the little movement ambles delicately along, seemingly (but not quite) unaware of its own insubstantiality. It is followed by another small piece, *Allegretto vivo*, in (or rather, around) B minor (subdominant minor of F sharp), which is even less secure, and the last movement inevitably is able to drive home B flat. This finale is not long, but it has tremendous scope and impetus, achieving a terrific climax at the finish.

The Suite is Nielsen's greatest piano work; it shows him at his most independent, treating the instrument with a forceful yet sensitive originality that throws off all fetters. He regards the piano as if it were virgin soil, and perhaps because he was not himself accustomed to routine techniques on the keyboard, his imagination treads few beaten paths. Nevertheless, he is no iconoclast, bringing the instrument to its knees with deftly exhibitionistic blows: he has by this time amassed rich experience of the deepest possibilities of melody, harmony, and tonality, which he applies to the piano freshly. The work is perfectly integrated, not a note too many, not one too few; like all his best music, it makes an impression of energy that is stark in the true sense, neither exaggerated nor understated, but pure.

Eight and a half years intervened before he wrote another piano work; then, in 1928, came the strangely compelling *Three Pieces*, published posthumously as Op. 59. These have almost the character of a tripartite sketch for a larger work; a first perusal suggests a certain laconic inconsequentiality, but familiarity reveals this as a sinewy contraction of thought. The first is an impromptu in which liquid *arpeggiando* writing alternates with contrasting sections of grotesquely humorous expression; its last part is marked *molto patetico quasi parodico*. The second piece, *Molto adagio*, has a directness and simplicity that is, at first, disconcerting; opening in a manner that suggests the middle movement of Op. 45, it falls from time to time into a cadential passage of childlike diatonic plainness, interspersed with more agitated matter: the effect is touching in the extreme, and the more familiar one becomes with it the deeper does it penetrate. The final movement is a fiery *Allegro non troppo*, short and concentrated, impetuously original in every bar; it is so close-knit and so unpredictable that a casual reading will not reveal any of its secrets, and only a mastered and convinced performance can release the astonishing force behind it.[1] No one should judge these pieces too hurriedly, and, as always in Nielsen, much may be learnt from his handling of tonality, which in this case gravitates towards E flat.

Nielsen's last contribution to the repertoire of the piano was characteristically friendly and engaging, *Piano Music for Young and Old* (literally, 'for small and big'). This is a collection of little pieces, all kept within the five-finger range; any one can play them, but they are by no means mere exercises. All are little jewels, utterly simple and straightforward, and every bar subtly breathing Nielsen's own air. No child could do better than to begin his musical life with these pieces, for not only do they fulfil the composer's aim of preparing an approach to great music, but they will remain fresh even when the pupil has reached old age. There are twenty-four pieces, in all the keys, in varying *tempi* and styles; no piece exceeds the limits set, yet Nielsen succeeds in delighting the ear time and again with unexpected harmonies, modulations, and fresh turns of melody, all within the range of a fifth in each hand. To single out examples for special praise is almost impossible, though there can be little doubt that No. 24 is the best of all, touching the depths in its E flat minor *Molto adagio*, which leads to an *Allegretto comodo* in the major, charming and unaffected as a nursery rhyme. Not one of the pieces is difficult to play, but any one who can do them all justice is well on the way to becoming an artist.

To end this chapter must come a brief discussion of the organ music. Nielsen turned his attention to this majestic instrument only at the end of his life: no doubt his previous neglect of it was due to his having had very little to do with the church; otherwise he might have rivalled Reger as the latter-day master of the organ, for his contrapuntal gift was ideally suited to it. Perhaps it was the encouragement of his friend

---

[1] I have Arne Skjold-Rasmussen to thank for a magnificent demonstration that enabled me to grasp this point.

Emilius Bangert, organist of Roskilde Cathedral, that led him at length to write organ music. His first attempt, the *Twenty-Nine Small Preludes* 'for organ or harmonium,' hardly promises much. Without pedal parts, often short to the point of perfunctoriness, sometimes lacking in character, most of these seem to have been produced almost absent-mindedly, and one would not easily recognize Carl Nielsen in many of them. Occasionally, of course, there is a gleam of light, and there is a general improvement towards the end of the book, the last four preludes showing much more of the real composer. But the main interest of this curious collection is in its occasional signs, in a progression here, a phrase there, of the coming of *Commotio*.

His choice of this title for his last great work is symbolic of the importance he attached all his life to 'movement' or 'current' in music. His very use of tonality is bound up inevitably with his conception of music as a reflection of vital processes; above all things he abhors that which is essentially static. Stillness or restfulness has its place in his art, but fixation of mind is for him synonymous with atrophy. In a sense this final work, written for the instrument with the most obvious ecclesiastical associations, is his testimony against the fixed assumptions of religious thought, in favour of fearless acceptance and development of life as it is perceived. If, in his last days, Nielsen wondered if his work had all been in vain, this was not because he doubted the wisdom of his own honesty, but because he saw the world's heedlessness to all forms of clear thinking; nevertheless, he never lost sight of the overwhelming evidence that such thinking is possible. Nothing could be more wrong than to suppose that Nielsen at the end was 'disillusioned'; he had never been illusioned. However, *Commotio* shows no signs of depression, and its grand spaciousness and peaceful strength mark the restoration of his confidence and courage after a period of difficulties. The work is by no means uniformly restful, but its total effect is of

that kind of controlled power that comes from a genuinely
serene mind.   He put his ideas about the piece in a letter to
Bangert, which is worth reproducing here; it gives a programme note for the performance in Lübeck, the occasion
Nielsen was never to witness.   The last two paragraphs were
written in German:

DEAR BANGERT!

  Thanks for the card! I don't rightly know how we should do the
programme, but we ought probably to provide the title *Commotio*
with a footnote, thus:

Carl Nielsen

Commotio * für Orgel, Op. 58

I should not like to have anything about 'improvising' in it.   The
work is so strict in form and counterpoint that I'm not able to make it
firmer—I could imagine the following if more is needed than the title,
which I would really prefer to be left by itself:
  The Latin word *Commotio* really applies to all music, but is here
especially used as an expression for self-objectivization (*Selbst-
Objektiviering*).   In an extended work for that mighty instrument
called the organ, whose sounds are derived from the natural element
called air, the composer must try to repress all personal and lyrical
feelings.   The task becomes great and strenuous and demands a kind
of severity (*Trockenheit*—'dryness') instead of sentiment, and must rather
be judged by the ear than seized upon by the heart.
  The work is supported by two fugues, on to which introduction,
linking movements and coda cling like creepers to the trunks of a
forest; but the composer thinks that further analysis is superfluous.

  * *Bewegung, auch geistig*, (C.N.), i.e. *Movement, also spiritually.*

Commotio is constructed like a Bach toccata, in four sections
—a *fantasia*, Fugue I, a slow movement, and lastly Fugue II.
To carry the analogy with Bach too far, however, is dangerous,[1]
and it is really more profitable to compare the structure of this
work with that of Nielsen's own violin Concerto, with its two
main movements, each prefaced by a slow introduction.

  [1] I flatly refuse to use the term 'baroque': the mere sight of a demisemiquaver
twiddle rouses many modern critics to ecstasies of scholarship.

M

Once more the essence of the whole lies in its search for a key; unlike the sixth Symphony's first movement, it finds it— beginning with a turbulent passage over a pedal G, it eventually reaches the noble key of C major, in which the second fugue is cast. It is perhaps significant that Nielsen's recovery of his old poise and strength results in a work that begins, like the first four symphonies and a number of works in his first two periods, with a great flood of tone, and it is painful in the extreme to realize that this rejuvenation was cut off so tragically.

The opening *Adagio* is, as stated, at first over a pedal G; it combines boldness of harmony with security and firmness of outline, and its temper is fiery. In a short time the pedal moves to the opposite pole, C sharp, a fact which results in the first 'fugue' beginning in F sharp minor (*Andantino quasi allegretto*). This section is not a fugue in the strict sense (its subject, for instance, has an almost 'Alberti' accompaniment, which, however, can be treated as a countersubject that in some measure anticipates the fugue's second subject); the sense of movement is, however, definitely that of a fugue. A second subject comes later, bold yet simple, with wide leaps and a Buxtehude-like freshness, beginning in G major. Elements of both themes are combined but, rightly (since this is not a finale), do not presume at a grandiose full combination; but the tension steadily rises as the counterpoint grows in vigour and resource, and the section comes to a massive climax in B flat. With a deeply impressive calming of the commotion, the key then returns to G, and the *Andante sostenuto* begins. This is, in effect, the introduction to the final fugue: it is tranquil, flowing counterpoint, among Nielsen's most beautiful pas- sages; it gradually becomes more agitated, but works steadily towards the key of C. The sense of expectation grows and there is a grand pause on the dominant of C; during this passage there are some wonderfully imaginative treatments of 'unrelated' triads.

When the C major fugue begins, it is in 12–8 time, on a swinging subject that is slightly anticipated elsewhere in the work (Frede Schandorf Petersen[1] gives two instances, which are undeniably true, though Nielsen does not 'evolve' the theme in any systematic way). The mood is joyous and calm and the progress of the last movement is easy to follow; there is a glorious feeling of infinite expansion and freedom from haste, and no one hearing this superbly affirmative music would think that it is by one whose time was running desperately short. Indeed, it suggests that its creator had all the time in the world at his disposal, that he was assured of a new lease of life. The fugal texture is not strictly maintained and there are episodes of more harmonic interest which serve to enhance the sense of constant expansion; the horizon is widened time after time. At a moment that is as hard to define as in a Haydn finale, a coda is felt to be in being; if one must mark the place, it would probably be at *a tempo ma fluente*, where all is marvellously calm and reflective before a trenchant *stretto* is built up, leading to a short but very final resumption of the fugal writing and a mighty climax. There is evidence that Nielsen may have wanted to expand this last passage of all, but whatever he thought can never be known for certain. It must be emphasized that the whole of the last fugue should be played at a *moderate* pace; to hurry it, or to lose the steadiness of its momentum, is disastrous. Given a proper performance, the whole immense work cannot fail to reveal all the finest qualities of Nielsen's mature mind; its clarity, its great mastery of the vast canvas, and most of all, its encouraging and constructive objectivity.

[1] See *Carl Nielsen: Kunstneren og Mennesket*, vol. ii, page 329: this is perhaps a suitable place to mention that Petersen's musical notes in this book are often of high quality, perceptive and scholarly: it is a pity that the format of the book (which is mainly biographical) has obviously cramped his analyses. It is frequently clear that he has had to truncate what might have been valuable essays on the music.

CHAPTER XII

THE HUMAN VOICE

A VERY large proportion (perhaps half) of Nielsen's huge output makes use of vocal resources: it would be no exaggeration to say that all his music is vocal in origin, in that its predominant singing quality springs from North European folk traditions (to restrict it to Danish elements would be an error). Thanks to him and to his fellow worker in this field, Thomas Laub, Denmark has become one of the few civilized western countries with a flourishing, living folk-music; this is also no doubt to the fact that the country has maintained its pastoral life—although during the past seventy years or so the towns have absorbed an ever-increasing fraction of the population, well over half the people are even now employed in agriculture or fishing or live in the country. In such a community, singing has always been an important social activity, and it is natural that its greatest musician should have made himself as indispensable in this sphere as he was in the instrumental. His contribution was, indeed, so extensive that a complete book would be needed to assess it: besides the two operas and several large choral works, and a number of 'occasional' works in extended forms, there are some three hundred songs of all types, from what suburban minds usually call 'art-songs' to the simplest, most immediately accessible folk melodies. Obviously it is impossible to deal with all this material in a chapter such as this, and it will be necessary to confine the issue to the most important works, the two operas, the *Hymnus amoris, Søvnen, Fynsk Foraar*, and the three *a capella* motets, with some general remarks about the songs, quoting in full the most popular of them all, *Jens Vejmand*.

It is convenient to begin with the choral works, since these show his vocal style in its most clearly analysable forms. The first thing that strikes one is the ease with which most of this music can be sung; Nielsen steadfastly refuses to treat his voices instrumentally, and any difficulties the singers experience are not caused by cranky twists and leaps in the vocal line, but by his often remarkable harmony and modulations which, once assimilated, can be felt quite naturally. Even in the distraught middle section of *Søvnen* (*Sleep*), the choral writing is concentrated within a normal range, and it is noticeable that at the moments of highest power he, more often than not, keeps the voices within their middle compasses; in this he must have learned some salutary lessons from Handel and Brahms. Choral writing, moreover, gives him ample scope for his mastery of polyphony, derived from a complete grasp of tradition, but always fresh and surprising in its effect. Torben Meyer gives the facts about the origin of the *Hymnus amoris*, which is virtually Carl Nielsen's first choral attempt on any scale (see page 191): like the first Symphony, which preceded it by four years, it shows not a trace of inexperience, and even if it were not known that the composer had spent uncounted hours in studying contrapuntal and choral technique, the fact would be self-evident in its results. Yet the music is completely spontaneous, and its sheer beauty of sound would be hard to surpass: the plan is simple and broad, in four main sections with a coda, each section dealing with one of the successive ages of man (childhood, youth, the prime, and old age), and the coda letting all four ages combine, with the help of angels, in a paean of praise. The text is in Latin. The whole work is based on a single theme of great beauty, given out, after a gentle orchestral prelude, by a children's chorus, 'Love gives me life'; the mothers join, 'Love gave thee life and thou growest in its leading-strings.' Ardent youth transforms the theme into a *molto animato*, 'Love is my aspiration and desire' (solo tenor and soprano); with the entry of the full chorus a climax is built, whereupon the full-grown strength of man is expressed in a striding *fugato* in march rhythm, 'Love is my spring, and deeds flower on its banks.' The voice of an unhappy woman interrupts, 'Love is my pain, nothing wounds me so, nothing is dearer to me,' but a women's chorus (*Amor est fons meus*) begins to echo the men's sentiments, the male voices join in a great climax of jubilation, and then the music dies softly away for the peaceful fourth section, in which the old men are heard singing, 'Love is my peace, my sunset.' Finally, children's voices (angels) enter, the full choral forces gradually come in, and the last blaze of triumph is generated; this coda contains some powerful harmonic sequences, but it is perhaps a little forced—Nielsen's introduction of extra-human elements is not really true to himself, for it is a romantic device. The final impact of the work might have been so much more real and touching if it had ended quietly, with the old men's philosophic calm. But this is the work of a young master feeling his own strength; as such it is a magnificent achieve-ment.

The next full-sized choral work, *Sleep*, came in 1904, just before *Maskarade*, and it is an impressive piece. In shape it resembles Brahms's *Song of Destiny*, moving from quiet to turbulence and back again. Johannes Jørgensen's poem, unlike Hölderlin's *Schicksalslied*, returns to its opening quiet, and it is not necessary for Nielsen to contradict the poet, like Brahms, in a consolatory orchestral epilogue. The two works have in fact no real common ground, for this is not philo-sophical, but plain description of human experience; yet, in contrast to what some would expect, it is much less subjective than the introspective Brahms piece. Its middle section, depicting the terrors of nightmare, seems subjective, yet it so accurately expresses what every one has experienced that it cannot be regarded as a merely personal utterance. The opening orchestral introduction is one of Nielsen's most lovely passages, not comatose, but wonderfully sensitive to those half-formed stirrings and thoughts that flicker soothingly in the mind as it floats out of consciousness; then the chorus enters, 'Kind Sleep, thou great mother, on whose breast we find refuge,' a long passage, *Andante tranquillo*, of glorious soft counterpoint. After this comes the harsh nightmare, 'Oh, anguish—Oh, terror! Woe is me! Am I awake?', *Molto agitato*, full of torn rhythms and distracted harmony; among many other details the cold repeated E flats of the glockenspiel make the dread sound of dropping water. Then it all fades once more into the calm of the first part (a masterly transition), and the work ends with a return to its original mood, not quite free from fitful half-memories of the bad dream, including *pp* repeated E flats on the glockenspiel (these may perhaps be regarded as a revelation of the real cause of the nightmare; who has not emerged from a dream to realize that what seemed like a death-knell was in reality the slow drip of rain from a gutter?).

Interrupting his work on the fifth Symphony in 1921 Nielsen turned (fulfilling a promise he had given) to lighter things in *Springtime on Fyn* (*Fynsk Foraar*); this he called a 'Lyric Humoresque.' One could not imagine him, like Benjamin Britten, calling such a work a 'Spring Symphony'; he took the symphony too seriously and mastered it too powerfully to use its name pretentiously: the sub-title 'Lyric Humoresque' is in this case a precise description of the work, as it would be of Britten's. This is one of the most Danish of all Nielsen's works, and it recaptures all the charm and fascination of that sunny childhood he described so perfectly in *My Childhood on Fyn* (some of which is quoted in Torben Meyer's chapter): the musical idiom is the simplest imaginable, folk-like and gay, picturing his own native environment with the kind of truthfulness and subtlety that come only from real vitality, however modest the aims.   Danish as this work is it would, with a simple translation of the rustic and touching words by Aage Berntsen, easily find its way into English hearts.   It is scored for moderate resources, four-part chorus, soprano, tenor, and baritone soloists, children's chorus, and a small orchestra without trombones—ideal, in fact, for the reasonably well-developed amateur musical society; at the same time, its gaiety and poetry are such that a first-class professional performance must inevitably reveal it as an exquisite work of art.

From time to time in his career, Nielsen wrote minor choral works for special occasions, some of which are still unpub-lished, and there is no space to discuss them here; one important addition to the repertoire of unaccompanied music must have mention, however, the three fine motets of 1929, Op. 55, written for that admirable musician Mogens Wöldike and his Palestrina Choir.   Many passages in Nielsen's music (both instrumental and choral) show, in their polyphonic technique, an elegant refinement and purity of style that betokens a deep study of fifteenth- and sixteenth-century masters, and it was doubtless his decisive rejection of religious doctrines that prevented him from writing much *a capella* music.   He once remarked that one could not write like Palestrina without his religious beliefs, and these settings of Psalms by David are straightforward human utterances; not even the quotation of a theme from Palestrina himself can prevent the music from being completely *Nielsensk* (this in the third piece, *Benedictus Dominus*, a quotation from Palestrina's *Sicut cervus desiderat* of 1581).   The first motet, *Afflictus sum*, contains the boldest dissonances, handled with severe consistency, and the second, *Dominus regit me*, is a serene contrast, giving rise naturally to the last, the most haunting of all.   Carl Nielsen's very honesty has its deep rewards, and the profoundest thing about these motets is the objectivity with which they demonstrate the subjective nature of religious thought, treating David's feelings as the natural outcome of the man's times.

Nielsen's two operas cannot be fully discussed in the English language until they have been produced on the English stage: of all European musical forms, opera is perhaps the most reluctant to travel; yet it is often the most intensely national works that achieve the widest popularity or critical esteem—witness *The Bartered Bride, Il Trovatore, Die Meistersinger, Boris Godounov, Pelléas et Mélisande,* and other works that seem to sum up their native origins in such a way that the foreigner is, for the time being, made to feel as if he were a Czech, an Italian, a German, a Russian, or a Frenchman. Nielsen's two examples are now part of the Danish national heritage; *Maskarade,* particularly, is inseparable from Copen- hagen's musical life, and would probably be cited by most Danes as the most intensely characteristic large-scale work to come from their country. *Saul and David,* its predecessor by four years, is also in many ways typically Danish, but its subject has a broad philosophical significance that links it with Greek tragedy rather than with any locality.

Saul and David (in four acts), with its penetrating characteriza- tion of the two men, comes from the same period as *The Four Temperaments,* having occupied the composer between 1898 and 1901. The libretto, written by Einar Christiansen, is extremely concise and effective, covering all the essential points in the famous story, and Nielsen's music has great nobility and strength: Saul, especially, is treated with deep insight, emerging as a genuinely tragic figure of considerable stature, instead of the somewhat petulant recalcitrant suggested by the bare facts in the Book of Samuel. One can feel Nielsen's sympathy for a man with the intelligence and courage to question things which, though he lives in a primitive world of superstition and savage unreason, he yet feels dimly to be a hindrance to the growth of the mind; but the force of circumstances and prejudice are too strong for him. His jealousy of David, the merciless vagaries of his moods, ranging from ferocity to noble magnanimity, and his eventual defiant death are all the result of a frustrated, conscious, and demonstrable superiority to all around him. David, on the other hand, has good looks, a disarming simplicity, physical prowess, and musical gifts: he lacks Saul's intelligence and character, but, unlike Saul, he is a born leader, for he shares without question all the simple superstitions of those who must be led, and he has what more than anything else angers Saul, a belief that the existing order is the best of all possible worlds. Thus the central figure, the real 'hero' is not David, but Saul, and his death has a tragic grandeur that makes David's final triumph fade into the light of common day. The music sustains a high level of inspira‑ tion throughout the four acts, and there is not space here to indicate more than a few outstanding moments. The very opening, turbulent and impatient, shows Saul chafing while he waits for the prophet Samuel to come and make the offering to the Lord; the character of the man, impetuous, virile, nimble‑ minded, leaps out of the music; not many operas begin more arrestingly than this. At the end of the first act comes the beautiful love‑duet between David and Mikal (Saul's daughter); it is richly sensuous without being sensual, and it has the same kind of innocent freshness as the love‑music of Berlioz in *Les Troyens* or the *Romeo and Juliet* Symphony. The brave and glowing prelude to Act II, the act in which David slays Goliath (off stage!), is the best of all beginnings to a concert of Carl Nielsen's works; with a real instinct for the dramatic, this act ends, not with the triumph of David, but with the jealous rage of Saul. Act III displays the incident in which David enters the tent of the sleeping Saul, but refrains from killing him; Saul's repentance and their reconciliation are celebrated in a superb polyphonic chorus, a monument to Nielsen's mastery of this art. Then comes Samuel, who lays this joy in ashes by anointing David king in Saul's presence. The drama of the fourth and last act is thus secured, and is driven home with unerring power and skill; the real depth of the scene in which Saul and Abner visit the witch of Endor may perhaps best be appreciated by comparing it with Verdi's much more melodramatic treatment of Ulrica's den in *Un Ballo in Maschera*. The real climax of the opera is, of course, Saul's cursing of God and his death; the actual curse is set in C sharp minor and rises, with magnificent defiance to a mighty and simple culmination in the major, at which point Saul kills himself.

Holberg's *Maskarade* is set in eighteenth-century Copenhagen, and its plot may be described simply thus: a young man, Leander, son of the burgher Jeronimus and his wife Magdalone, has been to a masked ball, where he has fallen in love with an unknown girl. But, as he tells Henrik, his cheerful servant, he is much depressed by his father's determination that he shall marry Leonora, daughter of a certain Leonard. After much mystification and comedy, during which both the young people insist that their hearts are elsewhere and that the last thing they want is to marry each other (this to their parents, of course), the curtain goes up on the third act, which is a masked ball. Leander and Leonora are both there and, being masked, recognize each other as the nameless chosen one; at last the truth comes out and all ends happily. Nielsen found for this comedy a style that is remarkably apt in at least three ways: it sparkles with warm humour, it is as Danish as Granados is Spanish, and it captures perfectly the eighteenth-century atmosphere without a hint of self-conscious *pastiche*. Many people still share Grieg's feeling that Act II is less convincing than the rest (see page 195), but the total effect is brilliant and gay in the extreme, with a lively sense of character and dramatic movement. The humour is light and never overdone, though comparisons with *Figaro* (which have often been made) are hardly fair to Nielsen, who always has the touch of a Danish countryman, and who is never so foolish as to try to change his own inimitable nature by adopting an unbecoming sophistication; he would have been the last person to agree that *Maskarade* is on a Mozartian level. What he does share with Mozart is his insight into character and his love of the underdog; there is no doubt that Mozart would have been delighted with Nielsen's treatment of Henrik, for instance. The orchestral interludes in *Maskarade* all lose a good deal out of their context, including the delightfully brisk overture; the best is certainly the lovely prelude to Act II, painting the deep and tranquil colours of nightfall.

Finally, how can one deal briefly with Carl Nielsen the master of Danish song? In this field his achievements are so varied and voluminous that only a separate study, giving translations of the many fine Danish poems that he uses, could do them justice. Such a study is clearly beyond the scope of this book. As a song-writer Nielsen is of high rank, and there is no healthy mood that he does not illuminate. In his own country he is best loved for his many folk-songs, plain strophic settings of simple poetry, often deeply moving. It is perhaps most fitting to end this survey, after ranging among his great concert and theatre works, by quoting the most popular of all his songs, *Jens Vejmand* (*Jens the Road-man* or *The Stone-breaker*): this is now part of Danish life and could easily spread to England. Its plain tune could be grasped by a child at once, yet it has a dignity and pathos that grow with each repetition. The poem is by Jeppe Aakjær (1866–1930):[1] in this one small song is all this poet's love of simple fellows, his deep sense of solidarity with those who labour to keep alive, all the directness with which his instinct finds what such folk need most. In this he and Carl Nielsen are at one.

[1] Translated by R. P. Keigwin (published by Basil Blackwell in a collection called *The Jutland Wind*).

Ex. 76

mf **Steadily, striding**

Who sits behind the | screen there With clouts about his | hand, his | eye with leather eye – shade, His | clogs with i – ron | band? That's | Ben, old Ben the | road man, Whom bitter need has | led To | take the stubborn flint stones And hammer them to | bread.

2. And are you roused at daybreak
    by something sounding plain—
    the clink of hammer ringing,
    again, again, again—
    that's Ben, old Ben the road-man,
    who stirs his ancient bones
    to hack the savage sparks out
    from morning's dewy stones.

3. And should you drive to market
    some sturdy peasant team
    and meet an aged toiler
    whose eyes are all astream,

---

¹ There is no prize for those clever ones who think they discover a connection between this tune and the *maggiore* section of the second movement of Haydn's 'Drum-roll' Symphony (No. 103).

that's Ben, old Ben the road⁄man,
   with straw round shin and knee,
hard put to ward the cold off
   and keep from frostbite free.

4. And are you wending homeward
   with shower and squall to breast,
while lonely Star⁄of⁄evening
   is shivering in the west,
and falls the clink of hammer
   quite near you as you fare—
that's Ben, old Ben the road⁄man,
   who still is sitting there. . . .

5. And so he smoothed for others
   the rough and weary way;
but as it drew to Christmas
   his arms they told him nay.
'Twas Ben, old Ben the road⁄man,
   his hammer slipped from sight;
across the heath they bore him
   one cold December night.

[1] 6. There stands within the churchyard
   an old decaying board
It's tilting badly sideways,
   the name is rudely scored.
That's Ben's, old Ben the road⁄man's.
   His life was full of stones,
but now he's dead there's not one
   to stand above his bones.

        [1] Last verse *pp.*

CHAPTER XIII

GENERAL OBSERVATIONS

VERSATILITY can be a curse to a man; it can, if he has no large purpose in life, torment and tantalize him. But a guiding purpose gives a man strength to select from his gifts those that can best serve his ends. Nielsen was versatile in a general way; he was a teacher, a conductor, a violinist, a gifted writer, as well as being a great composer. Married to a distinguished artist, he could not, with his perceptive mind, fail to become a sensitive connoisseur of art, while he read more widely than many a university graduate in literature. He did not, of course, have to select his life's occupation out of a number of con-flicting possibilities, for his musical creative gift far outweighed any other. But within this field he might well have been faced with difficult dilemmas, since whatever he turned to either became a great achievement or gave promise of outstanding qualities. It is as a symphonist that he is undoubtedly at his greatest; yet the string quartets show that he might have reached equal heights in chamber music. He tried his hand success-fully at almost every kind of music; he was a born vocal writer and his lively sense of human character and quick appreciation of dramatic situations made his two operas more impressive than perhaps he himself even dared to hope. Although he was not a brilliant pianist, he created an independent pianoforte style; in the field of song he could please the farm-hand as well as the educated Copenhagener. In his large works, his sym-phonies, concertos, and operas, string quartets and sonatas, he discovered and mastered a new and fruitful grip of tonality, and none of his contemporaries surpassed him in power of extended construction, while in miniatures he could, with a few deft strokes, strike the mark at once.

For an artist of such range, dilemmas must have existed; life was not long enough for him to attain all that he was capable of. The fact that such problems did not divert him, that he gained so even a measure of success in so many *genres*, is due to the clarity and precision with which his attitude to life developed. His progress follows an almost true straight line until 1922, culminating in the fifth Symphony; thereafter, until his last year, 1931, ill health, worry, and depression caused this line to waver, though it never really lost its continuity, and recovered its firmness at the end. Perhaps a better analogy than a straight line would be the outspreading shape of a fan, for the growth of Nielsen's art depended entirely on the steady broadening in the scope and objectivity of his view of the world. In all periods of his career, some inferior, 'low-pressure' works may be found; these are chips from the work-shop, but the major works reflect faithfully the expanding breadth and strength of his spirit.

It may perhaps be as well to summarize here what has sprung more diffusely from the analyses of the symphonies and the less detailed discussion of the other music; the careful reader will have already noted the consistent clearness with which a major composition by Nielsen expresses his attitude at a given time of life. It remains to indicate briefly how that attitude develops. First, like all healthy young composers, he is bent on asserting his own new-found powers, determined to show his skill and imagination. His first Symphony achieves this unerringly, but does not go beyond it: its use of progressive tonality is a demonstration of personal mastery and of that truest kind of artistic courage that can risk saying new things in old terms. This dynamic view of tonality (that a key is the starting point for an expedition to another key) is in any case characteristic of his own temperament, which cannot help looking outwards.

By the end of the first period he has reached the stage when he realizes that his own character both affects and is moulded by those of other people. What was instinctive is becoming conscious. *Saul and David* and *The Four Temperaments* both rise from the same impulse (indeed, the opera might well have been subtitled 'The Two Temperaments'); his awareness of other personalities now begins to balance that of his own, and his fascination for the analysis of human *types* comes of the growing objectivity of his mind. But he is still in the phase when his vision is confined to the separation and contrast of individual characters. Notice that, at every stage, what he sees is true; this is no trial-and-error, hit-and-miss process, for each step is an advance, in which he takes the facts that he has shown to be valid and consolidates them within the scope of a larger con-ception. That he now finds other people as interesting and important as he is himself does not mean that his own person-ality is less vital and real; but it no longer fills his world, and the greater mobility it achieves within these wider bounds actually enhances its true stature.

This generosity of outlook and sense of solidarity with his fellows naturally creates a period of well-being; *Maskarade* and the *Sinfonia espansiva* breathe a vivid gaiety that is created by no rose-tinted glasses, but by an irresistible sense in himself of the corporate strength of all the healthy-minded people with whom he feels at one. The symphony, particularly, amounts to a pointer towards the joyous, vigorous world that his experience leads him to believe possible; it has a certain questing, prophetic air; the obstacles that are in the way of what it seems to foretell are not yet, perhaps, fully perceived, though they are hinted at. His use of tonality as an evolving entity is here displayed with great power; the depth of his conviction that to move from one key to another is the essence of musical life [1] is amply shown in

---

[1] See his own revealing remarks concerning the 'current' of his music, on p. 186.

N

the third movement, which is the least conclusive of all four and is yet the only one to begin and end in the same key. This symphony shows one of the most felicitous faculties in Nielsen's mind, its way of perceiving its goal so clearly that it can express its character before actually reaching it; this same goal can still be seen plainly through the necessary conflicts of the next period. It is very significant that while the *Espansiva* opens with a great *allegro* in Nielsen's typical athletic 3–4 stride, the fourth and fifth Symphonies both *end* with such a movement, attained only after the most intense struggles. The conflicts of these two works, as well as the second violin Sonata (Op. 35) and the Suite (Op. 45) for piano, serve only to point to the essential realism that lies behind the *Espansiva*.

By 1914 Nielsen's outlook has widened to take account of life as an evolving biological process, of which humanity, arriving at consciousness, is the latest stage. The invincible will of life he finds proven by the demonstrably systematic nature of its striving, first for survival, then for development. His attitude must not be confused with Nietzsche's idea of the Superman, nor with those of Schopenhauer: Nielsen would never, for instance, have endorsed this comment from the latter's essay *On Genius*: 'Let us, then, not be surprised if we find men of genius generally unsociable and repellent. It is not their want of sociability that is to blame. Their path [1] through the world is like that of a man who goes for a walk on a bright summer morning. He gazes with delight on the beauty and freshness of nature, but he has to rely wholly on that for entertainment; for he can find no society but the peasants as they bend over the earth and cultivate the soil.' For Carl Nielsen the earth is made real by those who wrest life from it; he has no contempt for his simpler fellows, and in his most depressed moments would never have said, with Schopenhauer: 'I am

[1] It is surprising that at this point Schopenhauer does not say 'Our path,' for earlier in the same essay he says: 'We, the salt of the earth.'

often surprised by the cleverness, and now and again by the stupidity, of my dog; and I have similar experiences with mankind.' Nielsen's feeling that his cause is the same as that of the rest of his race does not stop him from making works of genius; it stimulates and clarifies his mind. Nor would he have agreed with Mr. Churchill's advice to Lady Violet Bonham Carter [1] on public speaking, that the most important thing is who you are, next, how you say it, and, *last and least,* what you say. An artist like Nielsen sees that 'what you say' and 'how you say it' are in fact the same in the finished work; but the content precedes the form in the artist's mind, which should be supremely superior to self-consciousness ('who you are').

The last section of the fourth crystallizes two dominant op-posed forces out of a welter, dawning consciousness struggling against what would retard it. The fifth Symphony makes this its starting-point, so Nielsen returns again to the special con-sideration of humanity: this time, however, he is not confined to the individual, but is concerned with man's great effort to understand and master his environment. He once described to a friend his feelings about this work and finely illustrated the human quest for objectivity by saying that he imagined himself wandering, indifferent, 'vegetating'; then came the desire to understand and belong to the world, and gradual consciousness of the purposeful harmony of things, with all the conflicts this new awareness creates in the wondering mind. In the second movement, decisive action is found, resulting in a full realiza-tion of the sense of unity with nature. This is his most powerful and deep-founded work, the essence of his mature thought, concentrated in a structure of scarcely surpassable subtlety and cogency, like a mighty challenge to all that is

[1] Quoted by the latter in the Lloyd-Roberts lecture before the Royal College of Physicians in November 1951, and later broadcast. The subject was 'The Power of Words.'

slovenly, vicious, destructive, or retrogressive. In it the *espan-sivo* element is made to take on new and deeper meaning.

Now the outstretched fan begins to fold again, the straight line to waver: illness brings about despondency and lassitude; the spirit at first wilts with the cracking of the physical frame. The sixth Symphony reveals all too sadly what was happening, and marks the low point from which recovery is very gradual. By 1925, the year of No. 6, he had been three years with the heart disease that he knew to be beyond cure, and though he tried to conceal it, a few of his intimates and family knew what it meant to one so robust and vital to be brought to such a pass. Nevertheless, he slowly cleansed his art of despair, in the touchingly sympathetic flute Concerto, the severely objective clarinet Concerto, and, finally, in *Commotio*. But there could be few new philosophical discoveries: the fifth Symphony shows the means, the attitude, by which a lasting and genuine expansion of the human spirit is attainable. Humanity at large has not yet taken such steps, but when it does (and Nielsen's conviction that it will is tremendously infectious), this man's greatness as an artist will be all the clearer.

Nielsen was no Beethoven. He lacked, among other things, Beethoven's superb aggressiveness, and his endearing, easy-going temperament prevented him from the ruthless, iron-willed concentration that made Beethoven unique. Yet he shares something with that giant; he is fearlessly honest, he is neither a 'romantic' nor a 'classicist,' his music is a funda-mentally affirmative analysis of human effort and achievement against odds (the finale of the fifth, for instance, is perhaps the only piece of its kind since the *Grosse Fuge* and the last move-ment of the *Hammerklavier* Sonata). Like Beethoven, he stands astride two centuries, and though his position in history is nothing like so clear and dominating, his influence can only grow.

The chief reason why Nielsen's influence must inevitably

be a healthy one is that it does not cramp those who receive it. His freely contrapuntal idiom, fresh in rhythmic and melodic flexibility, tends to free the imaginations of those who grasp its essence. Because of its very freedom, it stimulates the creative impulse without dictating it towards circumscribed techniques. In this he is perhaps in a better position than his great con/temporary, Sibelius, whose close/held, tensely harmonic style, based on a severely limited set of devices, has (through no fault of his own) tended to cramp many younger musicians into mere slavery. Every one is familiar with the composer who caps every work with the paraphrased climax of *Tapiola*, who potters about with woodwinds in thirds (with the inescapable twiddle), who can use the strings only for stark ejaculations or ground swells, who disguises the poverty of his themes by cloaking them in murks and fogs. None of this can be blamed on to Sibelius, whose mannerisms are personal and inimitable: one could perhaps criticize him for a certain lack of generosity in these matters. But it is to Sibelius's eternal credit that, at first a rather extravagant romantic, he fought a lifelong battle against this tendency, achieving greatness by one of the severest discip/lines known to any composer, mercilessly excising all but the bare essentials. His has been a lonely, single/handed fight. In this he is at the opposite pole from Nielsen, who never had to quash a dangerously luxuriant romanticism; he never had such a thing in him. His music is therefore based on positive, not negative premises, and can expand without fear. Such mannerisms as it accumulates are not of the limiting or cult/forming kind: it is almost impossible to write second/hand Nielsen, but it is exhilaratingly possible to let his music set spinning the mind's creative wheels.

His use of tonality has not yet been properly explored by others: many composers, of course, end works in different keys to those in which they began, but few have learned to evolve a tonality out of an extended process, or to regard it as capable of development in the real sense. It is quite likely that British music will find in Nielsen a real generating force: not only do his techniques and styles provide much that is still new, but his cast of mind, full-blooded yet utterly free from exaggerations, ranging from kindly humour to stern grandeur, capable of taut and compelling cogency of thought, powerfully constructive yet direct and uncomplicated, has all the qualities that appeal to most Englishmen. To say that his thought is 'uncomplicated' is not to suggest that it is not complex; a growing tree is a complex organism, but if it is chopped down and hacked into splinters it becomes complicated. At his best, Nielsen never complicates life, but he reveals its ordered complexities. For that reason alone his hopeful and encouraging genius will go on stirring new life in men's minds.

Carl Nielsen's eldest sister Caroline in 1879

One of the younger sisters, Louise, about 1883

Carl Nielsen—14-year-old military bandsman (1879)

The parents: Niels and Maren Kirstine Jørgensen, about 1889

A BIOGRAPHICAL APPENDIX

BY TORBEN MEYER

Translated by Harald Knudsen

I

To gain a real understanding of Carl Nielsen's music one should know something of his mind, and to know this one must consider the conditions under which he grew up: his childhood in a poor labourer's cottage on the fertile island of Fyn, his struggle to get on in life, and his ceaseless search for knowledge. His childhood is a special key to the under⁄standing of his character, and this first period of his life he has himself described in one of the finest autobiographies ever published in the Danish language, *My Childhood on Fyn*, which appeared on his sixtieth birthday in 1925. Born with gifts, as a toddler he already began listening to life around him, to mankind and to nature, finding joy in small things that nobody else noticed. The fertile field, the forest, and the bog were his playgrounds; lying out there on his back he was carried in dreams and imagination far from his everyday existence, and for any length of time he would stand and watch with great excitement the play of insects on the surface of a little lake. In these surroundings his sense of nature's rhythms was sharpened; this he kept and developed through⁄out life, so that it is natural that he, more than any other, should have created the modern Danish song. Not only was he fond of nature; he loved mankind in all its variety and, listening, he tried to penetrate beneath its surface. Already as a boy he disclosed a marked sense of dramatic point and conflict, a faculty that served him well in the great musical

183

works he wrote later, principally in his operas and symphonies.   More than in any other Danish composer his music
became a synthesis of all that mentally moved him.   His was
a dramatic and narrative talent of rare quality, enabling him
to derive great works from life's little everyday episodes.   He
could be an ironist, a lyric poet, a dreamer and realist, but
never was he a *fantaisiste*; he was, on the contrary, a faithful
servant to his art, seeking candidly to express what time has
proved of universal human significance.

Carl August Nielsen was born on 9th June 1865, in the
village of Nørre-Lyndelse on Fyn, about ten miles south of
Odense, where Hans Christian Andersen was born.   He was
the seventh child of the house-painter and village musician
Niels Jørgensen and of Maren Kirstine Jørgensen, *née* Johan-
sen.   The house he was born in had only two rooms, where in
nineteen years twelve children were born.   According to the
old custom the children took their surname from their father's
first name, in this case, Nielsen, i.e. Niels' son.   The Niels
Jørgensen family were extremely poor, so much so that other
people in the district often helped to keep the wolf from the
door, and it pained the mother to have to receive help.   Presents
of money embarrassed her, and knowing this the neighbours
preferred to give the children a little bacon, sausages, cakes,
and the like.

Both parents were musical.   Certainly the father was a
painter by occupation, but he much preferred his extra source of
income, music: he was an excellent violinist and played the
cornet even better.   The mother loved to sing.   'It seemed to
me that there was a rather sad sound in her voice, as if she were
longing for something far away beyond the farthest trees of the
land,' wrote Carl Nielsen in *My Childhood on Fyn*.   The
father belonged to a trio that played all over Fyn at various
local fêtes to the order of well-to-do peasants.   In the intervals
Niels Jørgensen amused the guests with all kinds of fun: he had

a great sense of humour and an ability to catch the fancy of others, a family trait that was inherited by nearly all the twelve children, specially by Carl. But Niels Jørgensen did not earn enough with his painting and music-making to keep a family on, so he took to farm-work and gave music and dancing lessons, and did many other things, so that he was often away from home for a long time.

When the children were about thirteen or fourteen years old they were sent out to earn a living, and consequently all twelve were never at home at the same time. Three brothers and two sisters emigrated to America, where the two sisters are still living. Two other sisters died of tuberculosis at an early age. In his youth Carl Nielsen was a slender, adroit, blue-eyed boy, with bristly, fair hair. He was quick-witted, with a keen sense of humour, and with his brother Albert he got up to all sorts of tricks. He had his own innocent way of passing time, and his powers of observation were remarkable for his age. A singing bird, a green wayside, or even a little striped fly could fill him with delight, and he easily spun his own dreams in his vivid imagination. Music came to him when he was only two or three, when he tried to hum his mother's little songs, and he loved to listen to the birds singing in the early morning and late evening. At the age of only four he first played—on cordwood: he had found that when pieces of timber were unloaded they made sounds and he quickly discovered how to arrange them so that they produced different notes when hit with a hammer. To indicate the notes he made crosses on some of the pieces and could soon play tunes on this 'instrument.' When he was six he got hold of a real instrument; he was in bed with measles, and his mother lent him father's three-quarter violin, on which he tried to find the notes she sang to him. After he got better he persevered with the fiddle and tried to play from music; the first time he succeeded he was so delighted that he ran to his mother shouting: 'Mother, come and listen, now I can play from music.'

A few days later she took him to Odense to the house of an old relative, where he saw a piano for the first time. On the violin he had to search for the notes, but on the piano 'they lay in long, shining rows before my very eyes; I could not only hear but I could see them, and I made one big discovery after another. I don't remember if I found chords or triads, but with one finger of each hand I played long rows of sweet thirds,' he wrote in his book. About this time he was set to do his first real work, to cut bricks at a nearby kiln with his brothers, and every Saturday they brought their pay to their mother, who thanked them with a pat on the cheek. In their free time they loafed about in the open, and Nielsen tells how he enjoyed the warm sunny landscape: 'There was a hum and buzz in the sun-dried grass of little insects and ladybirds crawling about or starting to fly. Some of us were on our backs with caps over our eyes, others on their stomachs as protection against the sun. It was as if all the world sang one fine tone, which made us all the sleepier when a bumble-bee or some other big insect whizzed by.' It can be seen how every-thing that moves captivates him, how his ideas first and fore-most concern motion. As he himself said in his latter years: 'If my music has any value at all, then it is in one thing, that it has a certain current, a certain motion, and if that is broken it's no good any more.'

When he was six he went to school in Nørre-Lyndelse and in his holidays he worked as gooseherd on a big farm. A couple of years later he was admitted to an orchestra called the 'Braga,' consisting of village players, school-teachers, peasants, and others, and here for the first time he got to know a higher form of music. His father and a school-teacher gave him violin lessons and one evening, at a harvest fête, he took out his first composition, a polka for the violin. His father disapproved

Enjoying a joke with Jørgen Bentzon (one of the most distinguished Danish composers, a pupil and great friend of Carl Nielsen)

of its syncopations: 'You'd better leave off such foolery—it's no good for dancing.' At this time his father also taught him the trumpet, which was useful to him in 1879, when there was a vacancy in the 16th Battalion at Odense for a regimental musician. Though he was only fourteen he won a competition against many older musicians, said farewell to his proud parents, and moved to town. As a member of a military band he became familiar with the functions of the orchestra and, of course, learned much music. He widened his knowledge with the aid of an old piano he bought on the hire-purchase system for a down payment of 50 kroner (about fifty shillings). In a beer-cellar young Carl met an old, underrated pianist, a man of some culture, who introduced him to the music of Haydn, Mozart, Beethoven, and ultimately to that of Bach. The door of a strange and entirely new world was thrown open to him.

As he became more acquainted with musical form he took an interest in chamber music and formed a string quartet with three fellow musicians from the band. The year 1882–3 saw his first chamber work 'Quartet No. 1.' It was obviously an imitation of the Viennese classics, and a Sonata for violin and piano in G major, a *Duetto* for two violins, a piano Trio in G, and some quartets for brass instruments, all date from about this time. None of these things have been published and they may be regarded as curiosities.

In May 1883 he decided to seek his fortune in Copenhagen: he got himself an introduction to the foremost musician in the country, the 'romantic' composer Niels W. Gade, who was head of the Conservatorium, and showed him the manuscript of his first Quartet. Gade looked it over with interest and told the boy he had a good sense of form and could enter the Conservatorium if he could also play the violin. In December he had an audition and was admitted as a non-paying pupil on New Year's Day, 1884. To take up this scholarship he had to have his parents' permission and that of the military authorities. Mother listened to him carefully; in his book he wrote: 'At such moments she was incredibly sweet, and her expression was at once serious, watchful, and sympathetic.' Father at first said 'no,' but when he realized that his son had made a serious decision, he gave in. Shortly afterwards Carl Nielsen went in the footsteps of Hans Christian Andersen from Odense to Copenhagen.

He studied there between 1884 and 1886, with violin and piano as his main subjects; he became an efficient violinist but was never quite at home with the piano. As well as studying music, he read a great deal, mostly Nordic and Greek mythology, Goethe and Plato, Shakespeare and Holberg. His favourite reading was Plato's *Republic*, which he kept at his bedside all his life. Some good friends gave him financial help. Besides his studies, he played the violin in a Tivoli[1] orchestra and elsewhere, so his time was fully occupied. When he left the Conservatorium there came three lean years, during which he had to rely on his friends' support and the fees of a few pupils; he continued to study with one of his erstwhile professors, Orla Rosenhoff, a theorist, and he joined a string quartet. In this period he wrote his first real works. To begin with there was a string Quartet in F (1887), which remains unpublished, followed by that in G minor (1888), later revised as Op. 13. In 1888 came also the G major string Quintet and the *Little Suite* for string orchestra (Op. 1). This last was his first work to be heard publicly, played in the concert hall of Tivoli on 8th September 1888, and was an immediate success. Six or seven months later the string Quintet was first performed, and was likewise well received. Then Nielsen won a competition for a post as second violin in the Royal Chapel Orchestra; he entered the orchestra on 1st September 1889, the start of a sixteen-year stay.

[1] Tivoli is Copenhagen's famous pleasure gardens.

Just before entering his new job he had written his little Op. 2, the two pieces for oboe and piano, and in 1890 came the F minor Quartet, which already expresses much of his individuality. Only the first movement of this Quartet was written in Copenhagen; the rest came into being during a trip abroad between September 1890 and June 1891, when he went to Germany, France, and Italy. In Paris he first met the young Danish sculptress Anne Marie Brodersen and they fell so immediately in love that they celebrated their wedding less than a month later. They visited Italy and then returned to Denmark. On this journey, after a performance of *Götterdämmerung* in Dresden, he writes in his diary: 'I admire Wagner and find that his is the greatest genius of our century. But I don't like his spoon-feeding of the audience; each time a name is merely mentioned one is invariably served up with the *leit-motif* of the person concerned, even if he has been long dead and buried. I find it extremely naïve and it makes an almost comical impression on me. I can't see that Wagner is hard to understand. That's just nonsense. He is easy to approach.' He never became a real lover of Wagner. Another note from the diary: 'I've come to the conclusion that Weber will be forgotten in a hundred years' time. There is something jelly-like about a lot of his things. It is a fact that he who brandishes the hardest fist will be remembered longest. Beethoven, Michelangelo, Bach, Berlioz, Rembrandt, Shakespeare, Goethe, Henrik Ibsen, 'and' the like have all given their time a black eye.'

The young Mrs. Carl Nielsen was in Paris studying sculpture. She was handsome, fairly tall, elegant, with a marble-fair complexion, blue eyes, and hair golden as ripe corn. Her whole manner suggested much dignity and purity of character. She was twenty-seven when they met, he twenty-five, rather stocky and well built. He had at that time a trace of shyness, his face was youthful and his dress modest:

his voice could be soft and halting, as if from diffidence. But under the bristly hair and broad forehead were his strong blue eyes, alive with a fire that seemed to light his whole person when he enthused about something, a piece of art, an idea, or a person. He could make wise and striking remarks, risk daring opinions, and tremble with the keenness of his feelings when he was roused.

His first attempt at piano-writing was in 1890, with the five pieces of Op. 3, and in 1891 he wrote his first songs, settings of five poems by J. P. Jacobsen (author of *Gurrelieder*); these latter had an inclement reception in the press after a perform-ance at his first independent concert, but they later became very popular. His job as second fiddler was not always a pleasure to him: many of the operas bored him to death, but when it came to Mozart his imagination was fired: the Viennese master expressed to perfection all that to him was the essence of fine music, purity of melody, clarity of form, respect for the simple intervals, and freedom from the romantic bombast and senti-mentality he sometimes found in Wagner.

Shortly after getting home from his honeymoon he felt the urge to compose a symphony, and during the year 1892 he finished his first, in G minor, Op. 7, which he dedicated to his wife. Its first performance was at a symphony concert by the Royal Chapel Orchestra at the Oddfellows' Palace in Copen-hagen on 14th March 1894, under the baton of Johan Svendsen and in the presence of the royal family. It had a very warm reception, and the young composer had to step several times from his modest place among the second violins to receive an ovation. The symphony has since been widely played, and he always thought highly of it and never depreciated it as a work of immaturity.

Subsequently he wrote two more piano works, the *Symphonic Suite*, Op. 8 (1894) and the *Humoresque-Bagatelles*, Op. 11 (1897). The first of his two violin sonatas came in 1895, and shows his indomitable joy of life.   This period saw also the birth of his three children, Irmelin, Anne Marie, and Hans Børge.   His growing feeling of vitality is reflected in the E flat string Quartet of 1897–8, while in 1896 he had fulfilled an idea that came to him five years before in Padua, where he saw Titian's painting of a man killing his beloved in jealousy. Both Nielsen and his new wife were not unnaturally impressed by this, and she thought of making a relief based on it, but eventually found the problem insoluble.   But in his mind the germ of the *Hymnus amoris* slowly developed, emerging after five years as an important choral work in which he lets the various ages of life praise the power of love.   Before he began the sketches he asked a friend, Dr. Axel Olrik, to compose a text after a draft he himself had made: when that was done he asked another acquaintance, the philologist Professor Johan Ludvig Heiberg, to translate it into Latin.   While the text was in preparation Nielsen steeped himself in early music, especially that of Palestrina and earlier composers, and he worked in the process over two hundred counterpoint exer⁄cises in the styles of different periods, including that of Bach and Handel.   He gave his reason for having the text in Latin: 'My choice of Latin can be defended by pointing out that this language is monumental and lifts one away from too subjective and personal feelings, which would be out of place where a polyphonic choir gives expression to so universal a power as love, and one can also bear the text⁄repetitions more easily in Latin.'

Carl Nielsen's home at this time was very modest, for neither his post as an orchestral musician nor his compositions brought in much money: but no one asked for much, and the couple were very happy with the three children; they had, too, many friends around them, especially artists.   On 7th January 1893, he made his not very successful début as conductor; all the same, it brought him an invitation to write incidental

music to a melodrama, *Snefrid,* by the Danish poet Holger
Drachmann, but this was not performed until 1899, and
then only a few times.   In the meantime he met Brahms
in Vienna, where he also heard a performance of *Tristan
und Isolde*: among other things, he wrote in his diary—
'Wagner's characters undertake too little; they only talk.
They talk about what has happened, what is happening, and
what is going to happen, yet nothing happens after all.   These
human beings cannot act, and Wagner neither.   As a dramatic
poet he is nothing and as a dramatic composer also nothing;
as soon as he tries to express life and passionate emotions they
become tawdry.   As a lyric poet he is great, but with lyrics one
does not construct a drama; they melt away.'   Towards the end
of the century he grappled with his hitherto biggest idea: he
wanted to write an opera.

II

Carl Nielsen was always a man in whose brain ideas were
fermenting and wrestling.   This was plainly visible in his
looks, at once thoughtful and active.   He wanted something
more than merely to write notes.   These must have meaning;
a thought must be associated with every phrase.   Often ideas
came to him quite easily—yet they would get no further.   'It's
the undercurrent that's needed,' he often said, and that sometimes was a long time in coming.   For his first opera he
found his material in the Old Testament, in the drama between
Saul and David.   He succeeded in his intentions, and *Saul
and David* has since been described as the noblest and probably
greatest opera in Danish music, a work which, despire
its essentially Danish qualities, deserves to be known far
beyond Denmark's frontiers.   It was written partly at home,
partly in Italy where, at the beginning of 1900 he wrote the

second act at Rome and Pompeii. When the whole was ready, he delivered it to the Royal Theatre, where it had its *première* on 28th November 1902, the composer conducting. He was normally still second violin in the orchestra. Public and press were divided in their judgments of the work; some people were disappointed at not hearing an opera in the usual style and others saw in Nielsen the renaissance of Danish music: but the opera was given only nine times that season. It has since been heard regularly, and its following continually increases.

Three days later, on 1st December, he conducted the first performance of his second Symphony, *The Four Temperaments*, which he had composed just after the opera was finished, during 1901. Nielsen was antagonistic to 'programme' music, and it should be noted that the title of this symphony indicates human characteristics, not a story (as, for instance, in Richard Strauss's tone-poem *Till Eulenspiegel's Merry Pranks*). In his book of essays called *Living Music* he wrote: 'The programme or title must in itself contain a germ of feeling or movement, but never a crude description of concrete events.' Symphony No. 2 has been played all over Europe, and has always been one of his most popular works.

In the year following this busy time, Nielsen and his wife travelled to Athens, where she was anxious to study ancient Greek art, and he wanted to compose and study archaeology; the board of directors of the Conservatoire of Music gave him a room overlooking the Acropolis, so that he could work in peace. In March 1903 he began the *Helios* overture, inspired by the sun rising over the Aegean Sea. He put a note in the score: 'Silence and darkness—then the rising sun with a joyous song of praise—it wanders on its golden way—and sinks quietly into the sea.' The overture was not altogether well received at its *première* on 8th October 1903. Carl

o

Nielsen was becoming a focus of dispute in Danish music; he had a few faithful friends, but there were others who looked in vain for the kind of beauty they had come to expect from the romantics. Untroubled by adverse criticism, he at once began a new choral work, *Søvnen* (*Sleep*), to a text by Johannes Jørgensen. Here he reaches the extreme of what, for him, is subjectivity.

On the very day that *Sleep* was to be heard for the first time, he handed in his resignation as violinist in the orchestra; this was the result of several intrigues and disappointments, as well as the fact that the work irked him more and more. 'I've sometimes sat and wept because I haven't got a proper chance to compose—when I feel most inclined to write, I have to go to rehearsals; it will have to stop one day,' he said to his friends. During this last year the theatre authorities had some-times let him conduct (*Saul and David, Carmen, The White Lady*), and he hoped he might be able to continue as con-ductor: but on 11th March 1905, he was informed that his position as second violin would remain unchanged, the direct reason for his resignation.

Already towards the end of the nineties he had thought of writing an opera on a comedy of Ludvig Holberg (1684–1754), who was born in Bergen but who lived most of his life in Denmark and was virtually a Dane. In looking through Holberg's rich output, he stopped at *Maskarade* and sketched out a plan with stage directions. He then requested Dr. Vilhelm Andersen to write a libretto. After only fourteen days the first act was finished, and the rest came quickly upon it. Nielsen began to work at it during Christmas 1904 and continued (with interruptions) throughout the following spring, so that the first act was ready on 20th May 1905. Act II was written in three weeks, and the third was done during a summer holiday on the west coast of Jutland in July–August, and finished off in Copenhagen in September.

He delivered it straight away to the Royal Theatre, where it was accepted in November, even though at this time the overture had not been written (that was finished only eight days before the *première*) and the opera's ending was not yet quite worked out. The first performance, conducted by the composer, took place on 11th November 1906. It is considered the Danish national opera, and never leaves the repertoire for long. Time after time it has had new productions and while Nielsen was alive he conducted it himself. Among those present at one of the first performances was his friend Edvard Grieg, who afterwards wrote him a letter:

DEAR CARL NIELSEN!

Thank you for last night. It is an amusing and witty work you have created. The first act I grasped at once, the second less easily, but in the third I again got hold of the great lines, and as a whole I'm in no doubt that it is the work of a new master, who says 'Here I am!' What fine humorous art and what a wise economy in the technique! I was totally laid out with exhaustion at the finish of the opera. . . .

Maskarade has been produced outside Denmark only in Gothenburg and Helsinki. On the evening in October 1931 when Carl Nielsen died, the opera was being given at the Royal Theatre under its new conductor Egisto Tango. With *Saul and David* and *Maskarade* he reached two climaxes in his life. He was in his prime, and there is in the music of this period a rich fertility and depth, arising from his healthy Danish mind and informed by the technical mastery that followed his artistic ripening. He composed quickly and easily, yet with strict clarity and an unfailing power of organization, and his original primitive feeling for nature gave him a sense of identity with the Danish soil, an indefinable sense that is also found in Hans Christian Andersen. In neither of these men is seriousness far from jocularity, but their solemnity does not walk in heavy boots, and their humour is not platitudinous.

His easy technical mastery at this time is well shown in the F major string Quartet, which he wrote while he was waiting to get *Maskarade* performed. Its tonal freedom did not exactly please the taste of the day, but simultaneously with such 'modern' works he wrote some very easily assimilated songs, such as the very popular *Jens Vejmand* (*The Stone-breaker*).[1] The public and press showed some confusion. In addition came a song that was soon taken into the collection of Danish national songs, *Du Danske Mand* (*Thou Danish Man*), with words by Holger Drachmann. This song will be sung as long as Denmark exists, thanks to its outspoken rhythm and because it is so very singable. In 1908 he completed *Saga-Drøm*, the first of his three orchestral tone-poems.

In the year after Johan Svendsen retired from his post as conductor of the Royal Theatre. Carl Nielsen had by this time become so well known that he was invited to take over the post, and he did so from 1st August 1908, on an equal footing with Frederik Rung, who had conducted at the theatre for some years. Nielsen stayed in this responsible position for six years, no easy time for him, since he was much more a creative than a re-creative artist. He had certainly conducted his own music excellently, both in the theatre and the concert hall, but now he was faced with the works of others, and these did not always interest him. He had never studied conducting and it occasionally happened that, during a performance, he would become absent-minded, lost in his own thoughts. But when an opera captivated him, he tackled it with enthusiasm; this applied first and foremost to Mozart, and also to Puccini and others. Soon after he entered this post, he was strongly criticized for his performance of *Die Meistersinger*, and not long after this he missed a beat in *Mignon* and created confusion; he was overcome with nerves and had to go home and let Rung conduct the rest of the opera. These

[1] Quoted on pp. 173-4.

episodes taught him how to keep a level head, but it was altogether a troubled time, even after he became an experienced
conductor.

III

In spite of all these difficulties he managed, surprisingly
enough, to create some of his most celebrated works, including
the *Sinfonia espansiva* and the violin Concerto. The up-
standing strength of the symphony, written in 1910–11 at
a time when, as a conductor, he was exposed to attacks and
adversities, might be interpreted as an answer to his antago-
nists: but a knowledge of his views as an artist leads to the
contrary supposition.   He was, of course, an artist with strong
feelings and a receptive mind, but he never worked under the
direct influence of momentary impulses or moods.   He could
be depressed or serious and still compose a lively song, and in
a cheerful mood he could write a serious quartet movement.
His creative faculty could separate itself from the petty distrac-
tions of life and he several times remarked: 'What business
have other people with my innermost feelings?'   This must
not be understood to mean that art should be unconnected
with emotion; on the contrary.   Passing feelings must be of
secondary importance, and the composer ought therefore not
to write rashly, on momentary impulses.   What Nielsen felt
and thought had first to go through a deep-laid process of
clarification, and not until this process was over was the
material ripe for its transformation into art.

He never made extensive sketches for his symphonies: his
forms grew gradually into wholes from cloudy conceptions.
They seemed to come of their own accord and he felt that while
he was giving of his utmost, nothing could go completely
wrong.   When he once became absorbed, he worked under
an immense pressure from inside that cut out all external

influences for the time being. Everything became insignificant except the creative process, and for a man like Nielsen this was indeed a fortunate ability, for otherwise his work might have fared ill in his often disturbed life. Even in his last years, when he was a sick man, he was able to produce music in which never a single note betrays his body's frailty, but which instead gives proof of a strength and wealth of imagination that is in sharp contrast to outward circumstances.

He once made a statement to the Norwegian newspaper *Verdens Gang*, giving an idea of what he wanted to express in the form and technique of the *Sinfonia espansiva*: 'I am—or better—I was often a bone of contention . . . but that was because I wanted to protest against the typical Danish soft smoothing over. I want stronger rhythms and more advanced harmony.' A Danish critic wrote about the work: 'It is the new dominant element in twentieth-century music, rhythm, that now makes its entry into the Danish symphony.' Once the composer himself called the third movement 'the work's heart-beat.' He thought of the main theme in a tram-car and wrote it on his cuff. The first two movements were written in the summer of 1910 at 'Damgaard' near Kolding in Jut-land, where he often stayed because it was the best place for him to work. In the same autumn the third movement was done: the finale he composed during the winter, so that the whole symphony was finished on 30th April 1911: it was first played on 28th February 1912. After much want of judgment amongst the Copenhagen critics during the period 1897–1912, he now met at last a different trend, and the work was received with open arms, a recognition that increased in the following years and secured him the central position in Danish music. Two months later the *Espansiva* was given at the Royal Theatre under his own direction, a unique honour that was repeated three times. On 28th April of the same year he conducted it in Amsterdam with the Concertgebouw Orchestra, and on 23rd January 1913 he conducted Max von Schilling's famous Tonhalle Orchestra in Stuttgart: a German critic called the *Sinfonia espansiva* 'a mighty animating call from the North.'

Immediately after finishing the symphony he began another major work, after an invitation by Edvard Grieg's widow, Mrs. Nina Grieg, to go to Norway to Grieg's country house 'Troldhaugen.' There, in a little hut where the Norwegian composer used to work, he wrote the *Praeludium* and the *Allegro cavalleresco* of the violin Concerto. The rest he wrote partly at 'Damgaard' and partly in Copenhagen, where the whole was completed on 13th December of the same year. It has often been suggested that the stylistic difference between the two main parts of the work is so great that they cannot be said to make a whole. Dohnányi, the Hungarian composer, thought so, and when Nielsen heard about it he wrote to his son-in-law Telmányi: 'We might perhaps say that the first movement is more lively and full of temperament, but is it therefore better music? I think not, and I took special pains to emphasize in the rondo that the *milieu* has now changed, and the very end renounces everything that might dazzle or impress. It seems to me that this is expressed as clearly as possible. It would have been an easy matter to finish brilliantly, but—well, it may have been stupid of me.' This work had its first performance at the same concert as the *Sinfonia espansiva*, and during the summer of 1912 he wrote another important piece, the second of his two sonatas for violin and piano, Op. 35.

He did very little more composition during these years, for the work at the Royal Theatre very much occupied his time. His relations with his fellow conductor, Frederik Rung, grew difficult, and Nielsen suffered many disappointments, until Rung departed this life in January 1914. The theatre authorities then brought in Georg Høberg; he was at once met

with such extravagant favour that Nielsen felt himself dis-
regarded and tendered his resignation. He left the theatre
after six years of service on 30th May 1914.

That Carl Nielsen can be called the great Danish folk
composer is less due to his great works in chamber music,
symphony, or opera than to his re-creation of the Danish folk-
song begun a few years after the turn of the century. This
work brought him for some time into collaboration with a
composer who also had this aim, Thomas Laub, the organist.
They intended to popularize Danish poetry by giving it a
new musical setting, easily understandable and pure. Nielsen
knew how to put a world of expression into even the simplest
song; usually the melody fits the verse so perfectly that it
seems to spring from the poet's words. He never forced the
tune on to the poetry against its rhythm, but released what
was latent in the music of the language and turned it into
living melody. In the course of time he wrote several hundred
Danish songs and hymns, from church melodies to cheerful
little romances, from poignant national songs to pastoral
lyrics. The climax of his work with Laub was the *Folke-
højskolens Melodibog* (a song book for the People's High
Schools). Singing has always taken an important place in
the high-school movement, but about the time of the First
World War it was felt that a new spirit was needed. Together
with two gifted pupils they created a collection of melodies
which, as well as the best of older composers' songs, included
many of their own, Laub contributing 158 and Nielsen
about 50. The song book brought a treasure of healthy,
typically Danish songs into the high schools and, furthermore,
to the people. It is one of the foundations of Danish popular
song, a book that is repeatedly reissued and is always in step
with the times.

Meanwhile Nielsen had become conductor of the *Musik-
föreningen* (Music Society) in Copenhagen, which was founded in

1836 and had Niels W. Gade as conductor from 1850 to 1890. From 1915 onwards he gave some six to eight concerts each winter, the programmes consisting of both old and new works, and he continued this valuable work until 1927, when he felt too weak to go on.   This position gave him plenty of time for composition, which he took up again as soon as he had resigned from the Royal Theatre.   In the summer of 1914 he was already thinking about a fourth Symphony.

In *Living Music* he lets music speak for itself:

> I am everywhere and nowhere.   I leap over the wave and over the top of the forest, I sit in the throat of the savage, on the foot of the negro, and sleep in stone and ringing ore.   None can catch me; all can grasp me.   I live ten times more intensely than anything alive, and die ten times deeper.   I love the great plain of Silence and it is my greatest joy to invade it.   I know nothing of sorrow and jubilation, gaiety and weeping, but I can rejoice, cry, laugh, and lament at the same time and eternally.

He opines that music must not be treated as a mere snapshot of a passing mood; it must go far deeper and higher, find, in fact, the innermost kernel, life's fundamental spark.   'What is music?' he asks and answers: rhythm and tone; but, he adds, aren't movement and sound the most elementary expres-sions of life's will and its indomitable craving to be free and independent?   Music is the sound of life; it is life, subject to laws of evolution and transformation, but invincible.   These thoughts were crystallized into the phrase: 'Music is life, and, like it, inextinguishable,' which became the motto for the new symphony.   Thus it is not a 'programme,' but simply a guide to the proper function of music as he conceived it, and he used a title only to help prepare the ordinary listener for the symphony.

He began the work in the summer of 1915 and finished it on 14th January 1916, only a fortnight before the first performance.

It was received enthusiastically; only the drums in the last movement caused some consternation and argument. Not only was the Danish musical world conquered; he was also sent for abroad, and became a member of the Swedish Academy, of the *Akademie der Künste* in Berlin, and several others.

The year 1916 was full of work. He returned to the piano, which he had neglected, and in 1916–17 wrote the *Chaconne*, Op. 32, and the *Theme with Variations*, Op. 40; in 1919 came the Suite, Op. 45, written partly during his summer holiday on Skagen (the most northerly point of Denmark), and partly in Gothenburg, Sweden, where after 1918 he spent several months every year conducting the orchestra of the *Konsert-förening*, alternating with the composer and pianist Wilhelm Stenhammar. In this way he created for himself a regular audience, and since then there has always been a special place for his music in Sweden.

Nielsen was now at the height of his powers. That he was conscious of his worth as a composer is certain, though he hardly said anything to that effect. His personal address was modest, but distinguished and dignified, and fame and popularity made no difference to it. He did not look at life merely through artistic spectacles; as a man he was too humanly interested in the many-sided struggle for existence for that. He could benefit from any discussions with intelligent people, and was often influenced by the opinions of others; but it was characteristic that he never attempted to draw attention to the details of his own works, or to analyse them. Such matters concerned only himself, and rather than explain them he would pass them off with a little smile.

In his Danish way he would often smile; he was open and light-hearted, and his sense of humour was without sting or malice. His knowledge of music, literature, and art was never used to advertise his intellect; he was not what is usually called 'slick,' but it is remarkable how easily (thanks to his charm) he won the confidence of all who came into contact with him. It was always difficult to say 'no' to him, and just as hard for him to refuse requests, so he had therefore many friends and admirers, so many that he had difficulty in coping with them. His natural grace and friendliness sometimes led people to expect more than he actually intended and he occasionally caused disappointments. But there were always others ready to be won over, and he was much loved and respected.

Besides the piano works, he wrote in these years music for plays at the Royal Theatre; among these was *Aladdin*, by the Danish poet Adam Oehlenschlæger. He did not intend to write imitation oriental music, but wished only to lead the hearers' minds, by means of sounds and rhythms, in the right direction: that he succeeded is proved by the fact that his incidental music has outlived the play; it is often given in the form of a suite in the concert hall. His music to Helge Rode's romantic fairy-tale play *The Mother* (*Moderen*) was composed for the Royal Theatre on the occasion of Slesvig's reunion with Denmark in 1920. He wrote it while on a tour of Spain, and it contains a march and two songs that can be counted as national music (one of the songs is patriotic and the other is the delightful *Min Pige er saa lys som Rav* [1]). Immediately after this he began to work at his fifth Symphony.

In February 1921 he again felt a strong urge to tackle the large symphonic forms, and by 15th January of the following year he had completed his No. 5, again only a few days before the *première*, which took place on 24th January. He was incorrigible in the way he always left things to the last minute. The first performance made an overwhelming impression, though there was some criticism. In the same autumn it was heard in Berlin, where he gave several concerts of his own works in the hope of gaining some ground in this home of music, and in 1924 it was played in Stockholm, where it caused an uproar.

[1] 'My girl is as fair as amber.'

People fled out of the hall, appalled and enraged by the dinning side-drum and the 'cacophonous' effects in the first movement, but it must be added that it is in Sweden particularly that the Symphony has since won many admirers.

In the middle of his labours on this work he had to break off, as he had promised the Danish Choral Society to write *Fynsk Foraar* (*Springtime on Fyn*). He put all his childhood's heart into this. He was immensely industrious during this period, composing, travelling; he over-exerted himself. In May 1922 he had to go to bed and the doctor diagnosed angina pectoris, ordering complete rest: he stayed in bed for several weeks, and all he could manage to do was—to knit. He did, however, complete the wind Quintet before this illness incapacitated him.

In April 1923 he was invited to London: since Emil Telmányi (who had married Nielsen's daughter Anne Marie in 1918) was also about to make his London debut, Nielsen was thus able to include the violin Concerto in his programme; in addition he promised his son-in-law a new work, which turned out to be the *Praeludium and Theme with Variations* for solo violin, Op. 48, not finished until after their arrival in London. The orchestral concert was at Queen's Hall on 28th June; it contained *The Inextinguishable*, *Pan and Syrinx*, the violin Concerto, and pieces from *Maskarade* and *Aladdin*, and it was patronized by Queen Alexandra, who was, of course, Danish born. Nielsen could never speak much English: he said he knew only two words 'yes' and 'ivory' (the latter he thought sounded so jolly). He pored over a language-course 'English in a Hundred Hours' and eventually succeeded in making a little speech to the London Symphony Orchestra before the first rehearsal—'Gentlemen, I am glad to see you; I hope I also am glad to *hear* you,' he said, and all the players laughed. At this there was immediate contact. The day after the concert he had to have audience with the queen mother at Marlborough House; but he discovered that he had forgotten to pack his dark suit, and he had to borrow Telmányi's, which was rather small for him.   He couldn't do up the top trouser button. 'Never mind, I'll manage,' he said. 'I'll just keep my hand over it and no one will notice.' With bated breath, his left hand before his midriff, he stepped towards Queen Alexandra and he expressed his deep thanks.   After a while Alexandra's sister, the Empress Dagmar of Russia, joined the company and it was announced that tea was served. Carl Nielsen was requested to lead both ladies to the table: with an empress on one arm and a queen on the other he walked across the room, hardly daring to breathe for fear his partly undone trousers should be noticed.   But nobody seemed aware that the suit was too small.

In August 1924, he started on his sixth Symphony (*Sinfonia semplice*), which was to be his last; but before it was ready, he experienced his life's greatest celebration: on his sixtieth birthday, on 9th June 1925, the whole of Denmark paid him homage, and citizens of all classes formed a great torchlight procession.   The Symphony was finished on 5th December, only the day before the rehearsals for the concert on the 11th, in which the Royal Chapel Orchestra marked his birthday by giving the work its first performance; the sixth is dedicated to this orchestra.   On the occasion of his sixtieth birthday he made some remarkable statements to a newspaper: 'If I could have my life again I would whip all artistic whims out of my head and be apprenticed to a trade or do some other useful piece of work in which I could see a real result,' he said. 'I've never been able to live by composing.   I've had to be conductor, teacher—and now I have a state grant of 3,600 kroner a year.[1]   But if I didn't have that and if I hadn't had such a

---

[1] About £190 a year: the cost of living was, of course, much lower than now; 1 krone (slightly more than 1s.) would buy 10 cigars! (R. S.)

low rent, it would still be difficult to make ends meet. I always dissuade youngsters from becoming artists because it's impossible to make a living at it in this country.'

IV

During a trip to Italy he wrote the flute Concerto (still unpublished at the time of writing); this is dated *Florence, 1st October 1926*. It had its *première* at a Carl Nielsen concert in Paris on 21st October, but he afterwards revised the last movement: the new version was played for the first time in Oslo on 9th November. At this time he was becoming more and more interested in characterizing the individual instruments, his work assuming the feeling of chamber music rather than the more massive kind. This is, of course, shown in the wind Quintet, the Symphony No. 6, the flute Concerto, and later the clarinet Concerto. 'The flute cannot belie its true nature,' he wrote in a programme note. 'It is at home in Arcadia and prefers pastoral moods. A composer must therefore fit in with its gentle nature if he doesn't want to be branded as a barbarian.' In the year 1928 he composed several very distinguished works, and it seems as if he felt he still had much to express that was new. Typical of this phase are the startling *Three Piano Pieces*, Op. 59; but he denied having deliberately tried to be 'modern.' He simply wrote as he felt, and was scarcely conscious of any sudden change in his development. The *Preludio e Presto* for solo violin belongs to this new manner, and above all there is the clarinet Concerto. This was first heard at a concert in Copenhagen on 11th October 1928, and the reaction to it was at once divided into two sharply opposed camps, one full of overwhelming praise and the other expressing something near to abhorrence. Later, however, it has had a more general acceptance.

True to his amazing versatility he felt the urge to do some, thing totally different after these remarkable and exacting works; this was to write a series of studies for the piano. He found that there was nothing that could suitably be used as a change from the normal text-book material, and he ingeniously confined himself to the five-finger range. Altogether there are twenty-four little pieces. 'I have, of course, not exceeded the five-note territory in these little pieces,' he wrote, 'but have, on the other hand, tried within these modest limits, by means of modulatory and polyphonic elements, to prepare the way to the great literature of music.' This *Piano Music for Young and Old* was written mainly in January–February 1930, during a stay in Gothenburg.

From this he turned to something entirely different—church music, which earlier he had touched only in his *Psalms and Sacred Songs* (1912–16); this branch of music was to be the last to occupy him. It may perhaps seem strange that, with his marked genius for contrapuntal writing, he had not before been attracted to the organ; the reason is not easy to guess. But when, in 1931, at the age of sixty-six, he started writing a large organ work it was surely only one more outcome of his adventurous desire to explore. He was not religious in the real sense of the word. Before he embarked on this phase he studied (as he did before writing the *Hymnus amoris* and *Saul and David*) the music of the older masters, Bach, Buxte-hude, Scheidt, and Böhm, after which he wrote *29 Small Preludes for Organ or Harmonium*, Op. 51 (1929).

In the same year he had composed the three motets of Op. 55, settings of David's Psalms for unaccompanied choir, and to retain the strict sense of objectivity, he kept to a Latin text, as in the *Hymnus amoris*. On hearing these works from his last two years one would not suspect that they were written by a mortally sick man: there is a youthful strength, a freshness, and an openness about them, as if they were the products of a man

in the prime of life.   But in fact his health was fast deteriorat-
ing; though he tried to conceal it as much as he could, his
heart would not let him be as sprightly and energetic as before,
and he had to go nearly every year to Bad Nauheim or elsewhere
for a 'cure.'   His hair still bristled on the front of his head, but
the ash-blond colour of youth had given way to white.
Certainly his eyes could still glance clear and strong, his smile
had all its old warmth and sparkle, his humour could still
flash, and not many realized that he was subject to a serious
disease: but at intervals came the attacks, warnings of the
inevitable.   Whereas earlier he used to nip up the stairs like a
youth he now had to go slowly, with some difficulty.   Late
nights exhausted him.   When he was out on a windy day he
could scarcely talk, but at the same time he could travel without
discomfort in a car, or even do a bit of gentle ski-ing, and he
paid scant attention to the doctor's admonitions.   One thing
he had to reduce—his conducting; this was far too strenuous
for him, but in his ordinary life he was very reluctant to give
up anything.   Most patients with his complaint would, for
instance, have refrained from driving a car, but Nielsen drove
his Morris indefatigably round the town; nor did he worry
about taking an air trip.   He made very little change in
his active social life and refused hardly any kind of work;
accordingly, he said 'yes' when he was asked in the New Year
1931 to become principal of the Conservatorium in Copenhagen: already in 1926 he had promised to undertake this and
would not dream of breaking his word under pretext of being
ill or tired.   But that he was not quite happy about it is shown
by a letter he wrote to a Norwegian composer:

> Yes, it is an honour and a pleasure.   But the youngsters will keep
> bowing deeply and behaving obsequiously.   You will understand that I
> don't like to be stuck on a pedestal like any other object.

Immediately   after   the   appointment   he   went   over   to

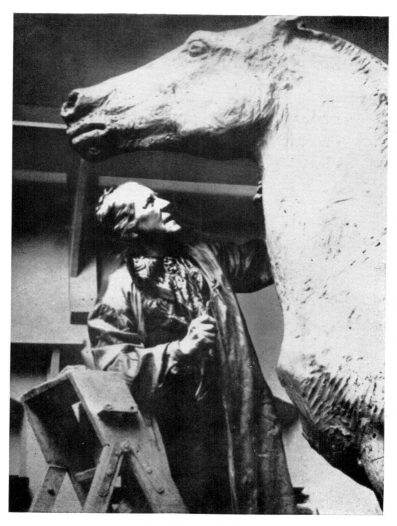

Anne Marie Carl Nielsen

'Damgaard' mainly with the idea of composing *Commotio*: from there he wrote to Telmányi:

None of my other works has demanded such great concentration as this: it's an attempt to re-create the one true organ style, the polyphonic, that especially suits this instrument, which has for a long time been looked on as a sort of orchestra: it isn't that at all.

It is typical that Nielsen, who all his life had renewed himself by prospecting fresh fields, should have ended with a work that strikes out on yet another path and is written for the instrument that has the grandest traditions of all. Towards summer it was decided that *Commotio* should have its first performance during the Nordic-German organ week in St. Mary's Church, Lübeck, and be played on 6th October by his pupil and friend Emilius Bangert. The composer intended to go himself to Lübeck, but it was not to be.

Commotio is dated 27th February 1931; then his work at the Conservatorium absorbed him for some months. But his heart attacks increased and he sometimes had to keep to his bed for days at a time, so he could compose only a few small songs. That summer he stayed with his daughter and his son-in-law, Professor Eggert Møller, in North Zealand; there in quiet hours he could open his innermost thoughts to his daughter Irmelin, and look back on his life and work. At such times depression was apt to come over him; what most disappointed him was the lack of understanding his music had met abroad. Unless he himself or some other Danish artist took the initiative his works were rarely heard outside Scandinavia. 'I know I've done it as well as I could,' he often said, 'but I wonder if it's all any use? Maybe what I want is all wrong. Maybe it's all nothing.'

In mid September he was back in Copenhagen, where the Royal Theatre was mounting a new production of *Maskarade* with Egisto Tango conducting. After a rehearsal Nielsen was standing on the stage, when there was some sort of muddle with

P

some ropes that hung from a high pole in the wings.   One of the stage-hands was unable to climb up to put it in order, but Nielsen, completely disregarding the condition of his heart, insisted on climbing up a rope to the very top.   Afterwards he and Tango made their way homewards together when it was clear that the strain had been too much for him; it had in fact given him the final blow.   He managed to be present at the theatre on 26th September for the performance of *Maskarade*, but felt so ill that he had to go home in the middle of the second act.   Two days later he was taken to hospital, where it was found that he had a blood-clot at the heart.   He was to have conducted a concert of his own works on the radio on 1st October, but the baton had to be taken by someone else, while the composer had to be content with a crystal set, so that he could hear the broadcast from his bed in the ward.   His own violin Concerto was the last music he ever heard: then he put down the earphones; during the night his condition grew worse, and in the evening of 2nd October he sank into uncon-sciousness.   The following night, 3rd October, at ten o'clock, he died quietly, while *Maskarade* was being given again at the Royal Theatre.   He was sixty-six years old.   The funeral service was held in Copenhagen's cathedral, and at the foot of the coffin was a great wreath from King Christian X and Queen Alexandrine; some of his own music was played and sung, and along the road to the churchyard the people stood in thousands to pay him their last respects.

His wife made a memorial, *The Singing Cherub*, which was erected in his birthplace Nørre-Lyndelse, on Fyn; she also created a famous monument, placed in Copenhagen, depicting Pan with his flute, sitting on a wild horse that symbolizes poetry.   In the rider's face one recognizes Carl Nielsen.

He was a renewer.   He became the driving force in Danish music, drawing together the threads of the past, purifying and sifting what he found, casting out what was worthless or dead, while he nourished new ideas and thoughts, fertilizing them by his rich understanding of the past. How fresh and full of character his music still seems—yet, like all great art, it grows out of the experience of bygone generations. He never self-consciously tried to be a 'pioneer,' but was always art's faithful servant, desiring only to express what time has shown to be of deepest and widest human value.

CHRONOLOGICAL SURVEY OF
CARL NIELSEN'S MAIN WORKS[1]
(compiled by Torben Meyer)

ABBREVIATIONS

Dania   = Samfundet til Udgivelse af dansk Musik/Ed. Dania (Society for the Publication of Danish Music/Ed. Dania, Copenhagen).

Sk. & B. = Skandinavisk og Borups, now Skandinavisk Musikforlag, Copenhagen.

W.H.   = Wilhelm Hansen, Copenhagen and Leipzig.

UP.   = unpublished.

PT.   = playing time (approx.).

P.   = see page.

STUDENT WORKS (p. 187–8)

1881–2. Sonata, G major, vln., pfte.   *UP.*

1882–3. 'Quartet No. 1,' D minor, 2 vlns., vla., vlc.   *UP.*
Duet, A major, 2 vlns.   *UP.*
Trio, G major, vln., vlcs., pfte.   *UP.*

1883–7. Var. quartet movements. Fantasy, clar., pfte.   *UP.*

1887.   String Quartet, F major.   *UP.*
1st perf. 25th Jan. 1888.

MAIN WORKS

1888. String Quartet No. 1, G minor (later revised), Op. 13, *W.H.* 1900.

Allegro energico; Andante amoroso; Scherzo, *Allegro molto;* Finale, *Allegro (inquieto).*
Ded. Johan Svendsen. 1st perf. 3rd Feb. 1889. *PT.* 25 min. P. 144–5, 148, 155, 188.

String Quintet (2 violas), G major. *Dania* 1937.
Allegro pastorale; Adagio; Allegretto scherzando.

[1] Not including the very large number of little songs and tunes scattered in many editions.

Ded. Thorvald Nielsen, Erling Bloch, Hans Kassow, Louis Jensen.
1st perf. 28th April 1889. *PT*. 30 min. P. 148, 188.

Little Suite, for strings, A minor, Op. 1. *W.H.* 1889.
Prelude; Intermezzo; Finale.
Ded. Orla Rosenhoff.
1st perf. 8th Sept. 1888. *PT*. 16 min. P. 8, 141, 144, 188.

1889. Fantasy Pieces, oboe, pfte., Op. 2 (*Fantasistykker*). *W.H.* 1890.
Romance; Humoreske. (*Romance* arr. for vln. and orch. by Hans Sitt).
Ded. Olivo Krause.
1st perf. 16th March 1891. *PT*. 3 min. each. P. 150–1, 189.

Symphonic Rhapsody, orch. *UP*.
Orch. 2–2–2–2–4–2–3–timp.–str.[1] P. 8.

1890. Five Piano Pieces, Op. 3. *W.H.* 1891.
Folketone; Humoreske; Arabeske; Mignon, Alfedans. P. 155, 190.

String Quartet No. 2, F minor (orig. Op. 6), Op. 5. *W.H.* 1892.
Allegro non troppo ma energico; Un poco adagio; Allegretto scherzando; Finale, Allegro appassionato.
Ded. Anton Svendsen.
1st perf. 8th April 1892. *PT*. 30 min. P. 145, 189.

1891. Five Poems by J. P. Jacobsen (*Fem Digte af J.P.J.*), Op. 4. *W.H.* 1892.
Sundown; In the garden of the harem; To Asali; Irmelin Rose; The day has gone.
(*Solnedgang; I Seraillets Have; Til Asali; Irmelin Rose; Har Dagen sænket*).
1st perf. 28th April 1892.

[1] The figures refer to the instruments in the usual order, as printed in a modern score; flutes, oboes, clarinets, bassoons, horns, trumpets, trombones (other instruments are noted by clearly recognizable abbreviations).

Songs and Verses by J. P. Jacobsen (*Viser og Vers af J.P.J.*), Op. 6.   *W.H.* 1893.

Genre Picture; The seraphs; Silk shoes on a golden last; That must be paid for; Song from 'Mogens'; Had I, Oh, had I. (*Genrebillede; Seraferne; Silkesko over gylden Læst; Det bødes der for; Vise af 'Mogens'; Havde jeg, o havde jeg.*)
1st perf. 28th April 1892.

1892.   Symphony No. 1, G minor, Op. 7.   *W.H.* 1894.

Orch. 3–2–2–2–4–2–3–timp.–str.
Allegro orgoglioso; Andante; Allegro comodo; Allegro con fuoco.
Ded. Anne Marie Carl Nielsen.
1st perf. 14th March 1894. *PT.* 34 min.   P. 5, 8 ff., 25, 28, 31, 32, 34, 38, 47, 115, 155, 165, 176, 190.

1893.   Music for *Snefrid* (play by Holger Drachmann).   *UP.*

Revised and expanded, 1899; dated 9th Feb. 1899.

1894.   Six Songs (Ludvig Holstein), Op. 10.   *W.H.* 1897.

You fine white apple blossom; Memory Lake; Filled with flowers; I walk in the sun; The gold and white heaven-light; Lazy fjord. (*Du fine, hvide Æbleblomst; Erindringens Sø; Fyldt med Blomster; I Solen gaar jeg; Det gyldenhvide Himmellys; Den dovne Fjord.*)
1st perf. 3rd Feb. 1898.

Symphonic Suite, pfte., Op. 8.   *W.H.* 1895.

Intonation, *Maestoso; Quasi allegretto; Andante;* Finale, *Allegro.*
Dated 1st Aug. 1894.
Ded. Victor Bendix.
1st perf. 4th May 1895.   P. 145, 155, 190.

1895.   Sonata No. 1, vln., pfte., A major, Op. 9.   *W.H.* 1896.

Allegro glorioso; Andante; Allegro piacevole e giovanile.
Dated 23rd Aug. 1895.
Ded. Henri Marteau.
1st perf. 15th Jan. 1896. *PT.* 22 min.   P. 16, 47, 145, 149.

1896. Hymnus amoris, soli, chor., orch.: text by Axel Olrik
(Danish), J. L. Heiberg (Latin), Op. 12. *W.H.*
1899.

> Orch. 3–2–c.a.–2 -2–4–3–3–tba.–timp.–str.; vocal soli:
> sop., ten.; 3-part children's chor.; 5-part mixed chor.
> Dated 27th Dec. 1896.
> 1st perf. 27th April 1897. *PT.* 25 min. P. 38, 145, 164,
> 165–6, 191, 207.
> Ded. Orla Rosenhoff.

1897. Humoresque-Bagatelles, pfte., Op. 11. *W.H.* 1897.

> How do you do?; The jumping-jack; The spinning-top;
> A little slow waltz; Doll's march; The musical box.
> (*Goddag, Goddag; Sprællemanden; Snurretoppen; En lille langsom
> Vals: Dukkemarche; Spilleværket.*)
> Dated 12th May 1897. 1st perf. 3rd Feb. 1898. P. 155, 190.

1898. String Quartet No. 3, E flat, Op. 14. *W.H.* 1900.

> *Allegro con brio; Andante sostenuto; Allegretto pastorale; Allegro
> coraggioso.*
> 1st perf. 4th Oct. 1901. *PT.* 35 min. P. 16, 36, 145–7, 191.

1899. Festive Prelude (*Festpræludium*), pfte. *W.H.* 1901.

> Ded. J. F. Willumsen.
> 1st perf. 4th March 1901. P. 155

1900. Cantata for the Lorens Frølich Festival (text: A. Olrik)
UP.

1901. Opera, *Saul and David* (libretto: Einar Christiansen):
4 acts. *W.H.* 1904 (vocal score only).

> Orch. 3–2–2–2–4–3–3–tba.–timp.–harp–str.; solo voices;
> chor.
> Dated 20th April 1901. 1st perf. 28th Nov. 1902. P. 5,
> 38, 169–71, 177, 192–3, 194, 195, 207.

Morten Børup's May Song (*Morten Børups Majvise*).
Come, thou white sun (*Kom blankeste Sol*) (text: Thura).
Dated 9th April 1901.

1902. Cantata for the Students' Association (text: H. Drachmann). *UP.*

Symphony No. 2 (*The Four Temperaments*), Op. 16.
   W.H. 1904.

> Orch. 3–2–2–2–4–3–3–tba.–timp.–str.
> *Allegro collerico; Allegro comodo e flemmatico; Andante malincolico;*
> *Allegro sanguineo.*
> Dated 22nd Nov. 1902.
> Ded. Ferruccio Busoni.
> 1st perf. 1st Dec. 1902.   *PT.* 30 min.   P. 5, 13, 21, 25 ff.,
> 45, 46, 47, 71, 101, 144, 146, 149, 169, 177, 193.

1903.   Overture, *Helios*, Op. 17.   W.H. 1905.

> Orch. 3–2–2–2–4–3–3–tba.–timp.–str.
> Dated 23rd April 1903.
> Ded. Julius Röntgen.
> 1st perf. 8th Oct. 1903.   *PT.* 12 min.   P. 6, 140, 193.

1904.   *Sleep* (*Søvnen*), chor. and orch., Op. 18 (text: Johs.
   Jørgensen).   W.H. 1909.

> Orch.   3–2–c.a.–2–2–4–3–3–tba.–timp.–glocksp.–str;
> mixed 4-part chor.
> Dated 10th Nov. 1904.
> 1st perf. 21st March 1905.   *PT.* 20 min.   P. 6, 164, 165,
> 166–7, 194.

1905.   Strophic Songs, Op. 21 (begun).

> *The Dream of a Merry Christmas,* fant. for pfte.   UP.

1906.   *Thou Danish Man* (*Du danske Mand*) (song by H.
   Drachmann).   W.H.   1906.

> 1st perf. 27th June 1906.   P. 196

String Quartet No. 4, F major (orig. *Piacevolezza*, Op.
   19), Op. 44.   *Peters* 1923.

> *Allegro non tanto e comodo; Adagio con sentimento religioso; Alle-*
> *gretto moderato ed innocente; Allegro non tanto, ma molto scherzoso.*
> Dated 2nd July 1906.
> Ded. G Breuning, Gerh. Rafn, Ella Faber, and Paulus
> Bache.
> 1st perf. 30th Nov. 1907.   *PT.* 26 min.   P. 47, 146, 147–8,
> 196.

Music for *Hr. Oluf, han rider* (*Sir Oluf, he rides*) (H. Drachmann). *W.H.* 1906.

Dated 15th Sept. 1906.
1st perf. 9th Oct. 1906.

Opera, *Maskarade* (libretto: Vilhelm Andersen after Ludvig Holberg) 3 acts. *W.H.* 1906 (vocal score only).

Orch. 3–2–2–basscl.–2–4–3–3–tba.–timp.–bassdr.–str.; solo voices; chor.
Dated 3rd Nov. 1906.
1st perf. 11th Nov. 1906. P. 6, 144, 147, 166, 169, 171–2, 177, 194–5. 196, 204, 209–10.

Come, God's Angel (*Kom Guds Engel*) (song by E. Aarestrup). *UP.*

1st perf. 30th Nov. 1907.

Song of the Siskin (*Sidskensang*) (song by E. Aarestrup). *UP.*

Dated 5th Dec. 1906.
1st perf. 7th April 1907.

1907. Strophic Songs, Op. 21 (I and II). *W.H.* 1907.

I. Must the flowers fade; The hawk; The stone-breaker. II. Lower thine head; The first lark; Homeless; Good-night.
(I. *Skal Blomsterne da visne; Høgen; Jens Vejmand.* II. *Sænk kun dit Hoved; Den foreste Lærke; Husvild; Godnat.*)
1st perf. 30th Nov. 1907. P. 172–4, 196 (The stone-breaker.)

1908. Music for *Forældre* (*The Parents*) (play by Otto Benzon). *UP.*

1st perf. 9th Feb. 1908.

Music for *Tove* (play by Ludvig Holstein). *W.H.* 1908.

We sons of the plains; Bird-catcher's song; Tove's song; Hunter's song.
(*Vi sletternes Sønner; Fuglefængervisen; Toves Sang; Jægersang.*)
Ded. Vilhelm Herold.
1st perf. 20th March 1908.

Music for *Willemoes* (with Emilius Bangert) (play by
L. C. Nielsen). *W.H.* 1908.

The ocean round Denmark; Vibeke's song; Fatherland;
Yes, take us, our mother.
(Havet omkring Danmark; Vibekes Sang; Fædreland; Ja tag os, vor Moder.)
Dated 30th Jan. 1908.
Ded. Helge Nissen.
1st perf. 7th Feb. 1908.

Saga-Drøm (The Dream of Gunnar), Op. 39. *W.H.*
1920.

Orch. 3–2–2–2–4–3–3–tba.–timp.–glocksp.–str.
Dated 1st April 1908.
Ded. Bror Beckman.
1st perf. 6th April 1908. *PT.* 10 min. P. 138–9, 196.

Music to *Ulvens Søn (Son of the Wolf)* (play by Jeppe
Aakjær). *W.H.* 1909.

1st perf. 14th Nov. 1909.

Cantata for the anniversary of Copenhagen University (text: Niels Møller), Op. 24. *W.H.* 1908.

1st perf. 29th Oct. 1908.

Evening Mood (Aftenstemning) (song by C. Hauch).
W.H. 1908.

1st perf. 19th Oct. 1908.

1909 Cantata in celebration of the year 1659 (text: L. C.
Nielsen). *UP.*

1st perf. 11th Feb. 1909.

Cantata *In memoriam* P. S. Krøyer (text: L. C. Nielsen).
UP.

1st perf. 4th Dec. 1909.

Cantata for the National Exhibition at Aarhus (with
Emilius Bangert) (text: L. C. Nielsen). *UP.*

1st perf. 18th May 1909.

1910. Music to *Hagbarth and Signe* (play by Oehlenschlæger).
W.H. 1910.

> Ded. Marie and Hother Ploug.
> 1st perf. 4th June 1910.

At the bier of a young artist (Ved en ung Kunstners Baare),
string orch. Sk. & B. 1942.

> *Andante lamentoso.*
> 1st perf. Jan 1910. *PT.* 5 min. P. 141.

1911. Symphony No. 3 (*Sinfonia espansiva*), Op. 27. C. F.
Kahnt, Leipzig 1913.

> Orch. 3–3–3–3–4–3–3–tba.–timp.–str.; vocal soli (sop.: bar.)
> *Allegro espansivo; Andante pastorale; Allegretto un poco; Finale,
> Allegro.*
> Dated 30th April 1911.
> 1st perf. 28th Feb. 1912. *PT.* 35 min. P. 5, 6, 12, 45 ff.,
> 66, 81, 87, 106, 124, 127, 135, 144, 148, 149, 177, 178, 197,
> 198–9.

Violin Concerto, Op. 33. W.H. 1919, 1949.

> Orch. 2–2–2–2–4–2–3–timp.–str.
> *Praeludium, Largo, Allegro cavalleresco; Poco adagio; Rondo,
> Allegretto scherzando.*
> Dated 13th Dec. 1911.
> 1st perf. 28th Feb. 1912. *PT.* 35 min. P. 45, 66, 124 ff.,
> 135, 149, 197, 199, 204, 210.

Song for the Children's Relief Day (*Bornehjælpsdagens
Sang*) (text: Johs. Jørgensen). W.H. 1916.

1912. *Nearer, my God, to Thee* (*Nærmere, Gud, til Dig*),
paraphrase for wind orch. *UP.*

> 1st perf. 22nd Aug. 1915.

Sonata No. 2, vln., pfte., Op. 35. W.H. 1919.

> *Allegro con tiepidezza; Molto adagio; Allegro piacevolo.*
> Dated 13th Aug. 1912.
> 1st perf. 7th April 1913. *PT.* 20 min. P. 6, 66, 71, 149–
> 150, 178, 199.

1913. Music for *Sct. Hansaftensspil* (a Midsummer Eve's
Play) (Oehlenschlæger). *UP.*

1914.   *Serenata in vano,* clar., fag., cor., vlc., cb.   *Dania* 1942.
      Dated May 1914.
      1st perf. 13th April 1915.   *PT.* 11 min.   P. 151.

     A Score of Danish Songs (*En Snes danske Viser*) (with
        Thomas Laub), Book I.   *W.H.* 1915.
      Dated 22nd Dec. 1914.
      1st perf. 13th April 1915.   P. 66.

1915.   *In memoriam* Franz Neruda, prologue, for recit. and
        orch. (Jul. Clausen).   *UP.*
      1st perf. 11th Oct. 1915.

     Carl Nielsen's Melody Book for Johan Borup's Song
        Book.   *W.H.* 1916.

1916.   Symphony No. 4 (*The Inextinguishable*) (*Det
        Uudslukkelige*), Op. 29.   *W.H.* 1917, 1947.
      Orch. 3–3–3–3–4–3–3–tba.–2 timp.–str.
      Allegro; Poco allegretto; Poco adagio quasi andante; Allegro.
      Dated 14th Jan. 1916.
      1st perf. 1st Feb. 1916.   *PT.* 37 min.   P. 5, 11, 66 ff., 85, 96,
      136, 141, 148, 149, 150, 157, 178, 179, 201–2, 204.

     A Score of Danish Songs (*En Snes danske Viser*) (with
        Thomas Laub).   Book II.   *W.H.* 1917.
      1st perf. 13th April 1917.

     Chaconne, pfte., Op. 32.   *W.H.* 1917.
      1st perf. 13th April 1917.   *PT.* 9 min.   P. 66, 155–6, 202.

     Prologue to the Shakespeare Memorial Celebrations
        (text: H. Rode).
      Published: Ariel's Song.   *W.H.* 1916.
      1st perf. 24th June 1916.

     Theme with Variations, pfte., Op. 40.   *W.H.* 1920.
      1st perf. 29th Nov. 1917.   *PT.* 16 min.   P. 66, 156, 202.

     Hymns and Sacred Songs (*Salmer og aandelige Sange*).
        W.H. 1919.

     Study after Nature (*Studie efter Naturen*) (song by Hans
        Chr. Andersen).   *W.H.* 1916.

1917.   Cantata for the Centenary of the Merchants' Com-
mittee (text: V. Rørdam). *UP.*

1st perf. 23rd April 1917.

1918.   *Pan and Syrinx,* orch., Op. 49. *W.H.* 1926.

Orch.   2–2–2–2–4–2–0–timp.–side-drum–xyl.–glocksp.–
tamb.–cym.–clappers–trgl.–str.

Dated 6th Feb. 1918.

Ded. Anne Marie and Emil Telmányi.

1st perf. 2nd Feb. 1918. *PT.* 9 min. P. 84, 136, 137–8,
204.

Music for *Løgnen* (*The Lie*) (play by J. Sigurjonsson).
UP.

1st perf. 15th Feb. 1918.

Music for *Aladdin* (Oehlenschlæger) partly *W.H.* 1919
(3 songs, Op. 34), partly *Sk. & B.* 1926, 1937,
1940, 1945.

1st perf. 15th Feb. and 22nd Feb. 1919. P. 84, 139, 141–2,
203, 204

1919.   Suite, pfte., Op. 45. *Peters* 1923.

*Allegretto un pochettino; Poco moderato; Molto adagio e patetico;
Allegretto innocente; Allegretto vivo; Allegro non troppo ma vigoroso.*

Dated Aug. 1919.

Ded. Artur Schnabel.

1st perf. 14th March 1921. *PT.* 18 min. P. 84, 156–8,
178, 202.

1920.   Music for *Moderen* (*The Mother*) (play by Helge Rode),
Op. 41. *W.H.* 1921.

1st perf. 30th Jan. 1921. P. 84, 141–2, 203.

Twenty Popular Melodies (*Tyve folkelige Melodier*).
W.H. 1921.

1921.   *Springtime on Fyn* (*Fynsk Foraar*), 'Lyric humoresque,' vocal soli, chor., orch. (text: A. Berntsen),
Op. 42. *W.H.* 1921.

1st perf. 8th July 1922. *PT.* 18 min. P. 6, 84, 108, 164,
167–8, 204.

1922. Symphony No. 5, Op. 50. *Borup* and *Dania* 1926. *Sk. & B.* 1950.

Orch. 3–2–2–2 (2nd doubles contra)–4–3–3–tba.–timp.–cym.–trgl.–tamb.–side-drum–clsta.–str.

Tempo giusto–adagio; Allegro–presto–andante poco tranquillo–allegro.
Dated 15th Jan. 1922.
Ded. Vera and C. J. Michaelsen.
1st perf. 24th Jan. 1922. *PT.* 40 min. P. 5, 6, 13, 45, 77, 79, 82, 84 ff., 105, 106, 141, 148, 151, 152, 157, 167, 176, 178, 179–80, 203–4.

Music for *Cosmus* (play by Einar Christiansen) *UF.*
1st perf. 25th Feb. 1922.

Quintet, fl., ob., cl., fg., cor., Op. 43. *W.H.* 1923, 1928.

Allegro ben moderato; Menuet; Praeludium (adagio)–Tema con variazioni.
Dated April 1922.
Ded. P. Hagemann, S. Felumb, A. Oxenvad, K. Lassen, and H. Sørensen.
1st perf. 9th Oct. 1922. *PT.* 25 min. P. 6, 105, 106, 151–2, 204, 206.

Four Popular Melodies (*Fire folkelige Melodier*). *W.H.* 1925.

Dated Aug. 1922.

Homage to Holberg (*Hyldest til Holberg*) (H. H. Seedorff Petersen), vocal soli, chor., orch. *UP.*

Song Book for the People's High Schools (*Folkehøj-skolens Melodibog*) (with Laub, Ring, and Aagaard). *W.H.* 1922 and many later editions. P. 200.

1923. Prelude and Theme with Variations, vln. solo, Op. 48. *Peters* 1925.

Dated 24th June 1923.
1st perf. 28th June 1923. *PT.* 15 min. P. 148, 204.

Christmas song, *The Heavens darken, vast and silent* (*Himlen mørkner stor og stum*) (M. Falck). *W.H.* 1923.

Ballad of the Bear (*Balladen om Bjørnen*), Op. 47 (text: A Berntsen after Almquist). *W.H.* 1924.

Dated 15th Nov. 1923.
Ded. Anders Brems.
1st perf. 13th March 1924.

1924. The Song Book *Danmark* (with Hakon Andersen). *W.H.* 1924.

Der er et yndigt Land (Danish National Anthem) (Oehlenschlæger). *W.H.* 1924.

1st perf. 1st June 1924.

Four Jutish Songs (*Fire Jydske Sange*) (text: Ant. Berntsen). *Sk.& B.* 1941.

1925. Music to *Ebbe Skammelsen* (play by H. Bergstedt). *UP.*

1st perf. 25th June 1925.

Symphony No. 6 (*Sinfonia semplice*). *Dania* 1938.

Orch. 2–2–2–2–4–2–3–tba.–timp.–glocksp.–trgl.–cym.–side-drum–str.
Tempo giusto; Humoreske, Allegretto; Proposta seria, Adagio; Thema med Variationer.
Dated 5th Dec. 1925.
Ded. Royal Chapel Orchestra, Copenhagen.
1st perf. 11th Dec. 1925. *PT.* 33 min. P. 5, 6, 45, 79, 105 ff., 127, 130, 162, 180, 205, 206.

1926. Ten Little Danish Songs (*Ti danske Smaasange*). *Borup* 1926.

Flute Concerto. *UP.*

Orch. 0–2–2–2–2–0–bass trbne.–timp.–str.
Allegro moderato; Allegretto.
Dated 1st Oct. 1926.
1st perf. 21st Oct. 1926. *PT.* 21 min. P. 6, 7, 121, 122, 127 ff., 135, 151, 180, 206.

New Melodies for Johan Borup's Danish Song Book. *Borup* 1926.

1927. Rhapsodic Overture, *An Imaginary Trip to the Faroe*

Islands (*En Fantasirejse til Færøerne*), orch.   *Sk. &*
B. 1942.

> Orch. 2–2–2–2–4–2–3–timp.–side⸳drum–bassdr.–cym.–str.
> Dated 6th Nov. 1927.
> 1st perf. 27th Nov. 1927.   *PT.* 10 min.   P. 139–40.

Vocalise⸳Étude, sop., pfte.   *Leducq,* Paris.

1928.   *Preludio e Presto,* vln. solo, Op. 52.   *Sk. & B.* 1931.

> Dated 28th March 1928.
> Ded. Fini Henriques.
> 1st perf. 14th April 1928.   *PT.* 12 min.   P. 6, 148–9, 206.

Clarinet Concerto, F, Op. 57.   *Dania* 1931.

> Orch. 0–0–0–2–2–0–0–side⸳drum–str.
> One continuous movement.
> Dated 15th Aug. 1928.
> Ded. Aage Oxenvad.
> 1st perf. 2nd Oct. 1928.   *PT.* 24 min.   P. 6, 7, 45, 122,
> 131 ff., 180, 206.

Bohemian⸳Danish Folk Tone (*Bøhmisk⸳dansk Folketone*),
paraphrase, str. orch.   *Sk. & B.* 1942.

> Dated 24th Oct. 1928.
> 1st perf. 1st Nov. 1928.   *PT.* 8 min.   P. 141.

Three Piano Pieces (*Tre Klaverstykker*), Op. 59 (posth.).
Dania 1937.

> *Allegro fluente; Molto adagio; Allegro non troppo.*
> Dated 15th Jan. 1928; 1st March 1928; 6th Nov. 1928.
> 1st perf. 14th April 1929.   P. 6, 158–9, 206.

1929.   29 Small Preludes, organ or harmonium, Op. 51.
Sk. & B. 1930.

> Dated Jan./Feb. 1929.
> 1st perf. 19th March 1930.   P. 160, 207.

Three Motets, mixed chor. *a capella,* Op. 55.   *Sk. & B.*
1931.

> *Afflictus sum; Dominus regit me; Benedictus Dominus.*
> Dated 15th June 1929; 25th May 1929; 28th June 1929.
> Ded. The Palestrina Choir and Mogens Wöldike.
> 1st perf. 2nd April 1930.   P. 6, 164, 168–9, 207.

Cantata for the Centenary of the Polytechnic High School (text: H. H. Seedorff Petersen). *UP.*

Dated 5th Aug. 1929.
1st perf. 30th Aug. 1929.

Hymn to Art (Hymne til Kunsten) (text: S. Michaelis), chor., orch. *UP.*

1st perf. 12th Oct. 1929. *PT.* 10 min.

Iceland (Island), recit. and orch. (text: O. Lagoni). *UP.*

Dated 29th Oct. 1929.

Land of the Future (Fremtidens Land) (song by Bj. Björnson).

Dated 28th Nov. 1929.

Two School Songs (text: V. Stuckenberg). *UP.*

Denmark, now the clear night sleeps (Danmark, nu blunder den lyse Nat) (text: Thøger Larsen). *UP.*

Dated 20th Dec. 1929.

1930. Piano Music for Young and Old (*Klavermusik for Smaa og Store*), Op. 53, I, II. *Sk. & B.* 1930.

24 five-finger pieces.
Dated Jan./Feb. 1930. P. 159, 207.

Amor and the Poet (Amor og Digteren), music for the Hans Christian Andersen Festival in Odense. (text: S. Michaelis).

Published: *In un boschetto,* Italian shepherd's air (G. Cavalcanti), Op. 54. *Sk. & B.* 1930.
The whole dated 22nd May 1930.
1st perf. 1st July 1930.

Cantata for the 50th anniversary of the Young Merchants' Education Association (text: H. H. Seedorff Petersen). *UP.*

1st perf. 3rd Nov. 1930.

Q

1931. *Commotio,* organ, Op. 58. *Dania* 1932.

   Dated 27th Feb. 1931. *PT.* 30 min. P. 6, 7, 79, 122,
   160 ff., 180, 209.

   Cantata for the 50th Anniversary of the Danish
   Cremation Union (text: S. Michaelis). *UP.*

   Dated 3rd March 1931
   1st perf. 30th March 1931

   Music for *Paaskeaftensspil* (Easter-eve Play) (text:
   N. F. S. Grundtvig). *UP.*

   Allegretto, 2 recorders, for C. M. Savery's School.

   Two Preludes, organ or harmonium. *Sk. & B.* 1947.

   What lightens over the field (*Det, som lysner over Vangen*)
   (F. Poulsen).

   Dated 23rd Sept. 1931

LIST OF MINIATURE SCORES

Little Suite, or strings, Op. 1. *W.H.*
String Quintet in G major. *Dania.*
Symphony No. 1. *W.H.*
Symphony No. 2. *W.H.*
Symphony No. 3. *Engström and Södring,* Copenhagen.
Symphony No. 4. *W.H.*
Symphony No. 5. *Skandinavisk Musikforlag,* Copenhagen.
Violin Concerto. *W.H.*
String Quartet in F major, Op. 44. *Peters.*
Wind Quintet, Op. 43. *W.H.*
Serenata in vano. *Skandinavisk Musikforlag.*
At the bier of a young artist (*Andante lamentoso*). *Skand. Musikf.*
Maskarade, Overture. *W.H.*
Maskarade, Act I (Facsimile). *W.H.*
Maskarade, Dance of the Cocks. *W.H.*

RECORDINGS AVAILABLE IN
GREAT BRITAIN [1]

Symphony No. 2 (*The Four Temperaments*), Op. 16. SSO [2] (Thomas Jensen) H.M.V. Z 7000–3

Symphony No. 3 (*Sinfonia espansiva*), Op. 27. SSO (Erik Tuxen) Decca AK 2161–5

Symphony No. 4 (*The Inextinguishable*), Op. 29. SSO (Launy Grøndahl) H.M.V. DB 20156–60

Symphony No. 5, Op. 50. SSO (Erik Tuxen) H.M.V. Z 7022–6

Clarinet Concerto, Op. 57. Louis Cahuzac and the Royal Chapel Orch. (J. Frandsen) Columbia LDX 7000–2

Overture, *Helios*. Royal Chapel Orchestra (Jensen) Parlophone XXD 8002–3

Little Suite, for strings, Op. 1. SSO (Tuxen) Columbia DDX 17–18

At the bier of a young artist (*Andante lamentoso*), for strings. SSO (Grøndahl) H.M.V. Z 294

String Quartet No. 3 in E flat, Op. 14. Erling Bloch Quartet H.M.V. DB 20100–3

Wind Quintet, Op. 43. The Wind Quintet of the Royal Chapel Orchestra H.M.V. DB 5200–3

Violin Sonata No. 1 in A, Op. 9. Emil Telmányi (vln.), Christian Christiansen (pfte.) H.M.V. DB 2732–4

Two Fantasy Pieces, Op. 2. Waldemar Wolsing (ob.), Herman D. Koppel (pfte.) Columbia LD 1

Æbleblomsten (Apple blossoms)
Genre Billede (*Genre* picture) } Else Ammentorp
Pagen højt i Taarnet sad (The page sat high in the tower) (sop.)
H.M.V. X 4574

Aftenstemning (Evening mood). Students' Choir (cond. Johan Hye-Knudsen) H.M.V. X 6344

[1] List compiled with the kind assistance of E.M.G. Hand-Made Gramophones, Ltd.

[2] SSO = Statsradiofoniens Symfoniorkester (Danish State Radio Symphony Orchestra).

Danmark i tusind Aar (Denmark in a thousand years). Aksel Schiötz (ten.), H. D. Koppel (pfte.) H.M.V. X 6631

Den danske Sang (The Danish Song) } Aksel Schiötz and
Havet omkring Danmark (The sea around Denmark) } H. D. Koppel
H.M.V. X 6605

Gron er Vaarens Hek (Green is spring's hedgerow) } Schiötz and
Farvel min velsignede Fødeby (Farewell my blessed birthplace) } Koppel
H.M.V. X 6988

Havet omkring Danmark (The sea around Denmark) } Einar Nørby
Irmelin Rose } (bass-bar.)
H.M.V. X 4573

Jægersangen (Hunting song) } Schiötz and Koppel
Vi Sletternes Sønner (We sons of the plains) }
H.M.V. X 6152

Jeg lægger mig saa trygt til Ro (I lay myself calmly to rest). Knud Eriksen (boy sop.) with boy's choir (cond. Mogens Wöldike)
H.M.V. X 4807

Jens Vejmand (The Stone-breaker). Schiötz and Koppel
H.M.V. X 6989

Sommersang (Summer song) } Schiötz and Koppel
I Aften (This evening) }
H.M.V. X 6987

Sommersang (Summer song) Käte Bruun Bielenberg (sop.), Folmer Jensen (pfte.) Columbia DD 511

Underlige Aftenlufte (Strange evening airs). Schiötz and Koppel
H.M.V. X 6610

Aladdin (Incidental music). Tivoli Concert Orchestra (Christian Felumb) Hindu Dance and Oriental Festival March
H.M.V. X 4676

Negro Dance, Aladdin's Dream, and Dance of the Morning Mist
H.M.V. Z 231

The Market in Ispahan H.M.V. Z 232

Maskarade. Prelude (Act II) Tivoli Concert Orchestra (Felumb)
H.M.V. Z 232

Overture and Dance of the Cocks. Royal Chapel Orchestra (Hye-Knudsen) H.M.V. Z 230

Magdalone's Dancing Scene (Act II)
Ingeborg Steffensen (mezzo), Einar Nørby (bass-bar.), Aksel Schiötz (ten.), with orchestra H.M.V. DB 5237

Moderen (Incidental music)

Min pige er saa lys som Rav (My girl is as fair as amber)

Jeg bærer med Smil min Byrde (I bear my load with a smile)

Schiötz and Chr. Christiansen

H.M.V. X 6065

Prelude (Act III, Sc. vii) and Patriotic Song. Royal Chapel Orchestra (Hye-Knudsen)   H.M.V. Z 237

Song of the Scald

So bitter was my heart

Schiötz with orchestra

H.M.V. DB 5241

Min pige er saa lys som Rav (My girl is as fair as amber)

Springtime on Fyn.

Den milde Dag er lys en lang (The mild day is light and long)

Schiötz with orchestra

H.M.V. X 6612

A few notes on the recordings of the large works may be useful. Of the symphonies the best performed are Nos. 2 and 4. Jensen has great vitality and a clear conception of the four distinct temperaments in No. 2, and although the recording is a little shrill, it is clean and well balanced, with a good solid bass; the performance could hardly be improved upon. Grøndahl's treatment of No. 4 is scarcely less fine (there is only the slightest falling-off of tension just before the recapitulation in the first movement—end of side 2—that can be criticized); the orchestra plays almost as superbly as it did in Festival Hall in Sept. 1951, and the recording catches most of the details, especially the two pairs of drums in the staggering finale, with only occasional distortion. Erik Tuxen has taken great trouble with Nos. 3 and 5, and the result in each case suggests too strict a caution; some of the composer's most characteristic effects are damped down for the sake of clarity when it might have been better to 'let it rip'; this fine orchestra always plays best when it is given its head. This is particularly true of the second movement of No. 5, which is held back too much, and consequently lacks the tremendous drive it should have; in this same movement, far more should have been made of the huge *allargando* at the end, on which the convincing establishment of E flat major to a great extent depends. But the climax of the first

---

[1] These two songs coupled with *I Solen gaar jeg bag min Plov* (*In the sun I walk behind my plough*) from Op. 10.

movement is finely done, with some magnificent side-drumming. The recording of No. 5 is clearer than that of the *Sinfonia espansiva,* which, though its sound is rich in the extreme, is inclined to be thick; No. 3 is beautifully played, though here again there could have been more rhythmic life. Admirable in some ways as are Tuxen's interpretations, their virtues (freedom from exaggeration, care for matters of balance and clarity) are apt to be negative ones, and I am convinced that if this conductor were to shed some of his restraints (not of gesture but of rhythm), the results would surprise and delight himself. The two voices in No. 3 are very fine indeed.

Cahuzac's performance of the clarinet Concerto is brilliant but inclined to be superficial; it is, however, beautifully recorded and is a valuable means of getting to know this work. A more sympathetic performance, however, might have made it easier for the average listener to approach this difficult piece of music.

Of the chamber works, the wind Quintet is best served: all the players except the flautist (who in any case knew the composer and was the first performer of the flute Concerto) are the original dedicatees. The recording is still reasonably good, and the playing is more sensitive than in a more recent recording (not, so far, available in England) by another group of players. The E flat Quartet gets a rather scrappy performance and several hearings are necessary before the work's essence can be perceived by the listener. Emil Telmányi is not at his best in the A major Sonata, which he plays in a lush, romantic manner.

Aksel Schiötz's many delightful recordings should on no account be missed.

Herman D. Koppel has recorded all the main pianoforte works; these are not (at the time of going to press) available in England, but ought eventually to be so, and the same may be said of Arne Skjold-Rasmussen's superb *Tono* records of Opp. 40 and 59.

R. S.

BOOKS:

Carl Nielsen: Kunstneren og Mennesket (2 vols.); by Torben Meyer and Frede Schandorf Petersen (*Nyt Nordisk Forlag, Arnold Busek, Copenhagen*), 1947.

Carl Nielsen; by Ludvig Dolleris (*Fyns Boghandels Forlag, Viggo Madsen, Odense*), 1949.

INDEX

INDEX

Page references to Carl Nielsen's works are included in the
chronological list (p. 212).

233